A CENTURY IN CEYLON

A Brief History of the Work of

THE AMERICAN BOARD IN CEYLON

1816-1916

CENTURY IN CEYLON

A Brief History of the Work of

THE AMERICAN BOARD IN CEYLON

1816-1916

COMPILED BY

HELEN I. ROOT

GYAN

Published by

GYAN

Gyan Publishing House
5, Ansari Road
Daryaganj, New Delhi-110002
Phone: 011-47034999, 9811692060
E-mail: books@gyanbooks.com

Distribution Network
gyanbooks.com
India, USA, Canada, UK, Australia, France

ISBN : 978-81-212-3205-0 (PB)
First Published, Amrican Mission, 1916

2nd Impression 2020

Printed at: Gyan Press, Delhi.

A Century in Ceylon
A Brief History of the Work of
The American Board in Ceylon
1816-1916
Author: Helen I. Root

A CENTURY IN CEYLON

A Brief History of the Work of

THE AMERICAN BOARD IN CEYLON

1816 —— 1916

Compiled by

HELEN I. ROOT

Published by
THE AMERICAN CEYLON MISSION
1916

A CENTURY IN CEYLON

I

1816–1821

"A land which the Lord careth for"

The first missionaries sent to India by the American Board in 1812 met the opposition of the East India Company and were ordered to leave Calcutta at once. Messrs. Judson and Rice united with the Baptists and found their way ultimately to Burma, Messrs. Hall and Nott received passports to Bombay and there established the first mission of the A. B. C. F. M. Mr. and Mrs. Newell went to the Isle of France where Harriet Newell died "without one regret at leaving her native land for the cause of Christ," and in Feb., 1813, Mr. Newell started as he supposed for Bombay but was landed, 'providentially, on the island of Ceylon. Anticipating that the brethren in Bombay might be

COAST OF CEYLON

forced to leave India, he decided to await their arrival in Ceylon, yet felt most unsettled as to his movements. "A solitary pilgrim in a heathen land" he spent ten months in Colombo, constantly preaching in English to the foreigners and Eurasians and gaining a knowledge of the situation which he passed on in urgent letters to the Board. He strongly recommended establishing a mission in Ceylon and for the following reasons:

1. The friendly and fostering attitude of the Ceylon Government. The Governor, the Chief Justice, the Royal Chaplain and many others of position

and authority united cordially in welcoming the work of missionaries among the native people.

2. The comparatively small number of inhabitants, somewhere under three million souls, all freely accessible.

3. The fact that only two languages were used and that in these the Scriptures were already printed, the whole Bible in Tamil and the New Testament in Singalese.

4. The fact that there were but two missionaries in the Island, one from the London Missionary Society and one from the English Baptists.

5. The remarkable opportunity offered for reaching the millions of Tamil speaking people in South India through the medium of a strong work among the Tamil community of Ceylon.

Immediately after the conclusion of peace between the United States and Great Britain in 1814, the Prudential Committee of the A. B. C. F. M. recognizing that very unusual facilities for missionary work were indeed offered in Ceylon, took steps to fit out a second mission designated for that island.

COLOMBO STREET

Mr. Edward Warren and Messrs. Richards, Bardwell, Poor, Meigs with their wives sailed from Boston in August, 1815, after impressive ordination services at Newport on June 21. The new Mission effected a simple organization on the way out, each of the brethren serving as President in turn and all meeting regularly for prayer, conference and study. On arrival in Colombo they met a touching welcome from English missionaries who had by that time settled in Ceylon, Rev. Mr. Chater, of the Baptist Mission, proposing to sing at their first meeting,

"Kindred in Christ, for His dear sake,
A hearty welcome here receive."

Governor Brownrigg granted them his gracious permission to land and reside in the Island, and after a few days, through the courtesy of the Royal Chaplain they were personally presented to him and assured of his protection.

It proved to be impossible to select a permanent location without more definite knowledge of local conditions than our missionaries possessed and they were glad to avail themselves of the aid of the Government officials in gaining information. They hired a house in Colombo, lived there together as one household sharing from a common fund, and for several months entered heartily into the English work of the missionaries there. They preached frequently in the Baptist Chapel, the Wesleyan Mission, and the old Dutch church which was maintained for the descendants of the early Dutch and Portuguese settlers. By invitation of the Govt. Chaplain they undertook the instruction in theology of some selected native young men who spoke English. They opened schools for English-speaking boys and girls, doing all this hard work without renumeration, to help the missions already established. April 21, 1816, they organized themselves into a Congregational church, thereafter holding communion services in alternation with the Baptists in their Chapel.

All this time they were carefully making inquiry looking into the permanent location of the Mission. It was determined to send Mr. and Mrs. Bardwell to strengthen the work at Bombay, while the others concluded on many grounds that Jaffna was the most promising field open in Ceylon and ultimately decided to settle there. The Jaffna peninsula extends into the Indian Ocean at the extreme north of the island, a garden spot, low-lying, of coral formation,

JAFFNA TOWN

rich in agricultural resources. The people are Tamils by race, and Hindus by religion, a comparatively isolated community, a third of a million in numbers, separated by Palk Strait from the Tamils of South India and by a hundred miles of jungle from the Singalese of the main island of Ceylon. Rev. E. Warren was the first to reach the field, on July 11, 1816, coming overland in a palanquin, a laborious journey through the inhabited central portion of the island and through long forest roads north to the old Elephant Pass, then over a causeway across a wide lagoon to the Jaffna peninsula. The others soon joined him and they took a house in Jaffna Town, the one small city of the province. Wesleyan missionaries from England were by this time established there, and this fact influenced the decision of the Americans to press out into the open country, thickly settled and wholly unreached by Protestant Christian influences.

The Governor, while prevented by treaty restrictions from giving them outright the lands and buildings set apart for the purposes of Protestant worship, encouraged them to occupy the ruined churches and houses at Tellippalai and Vaddukoddai, saying that "no part of his official duty gave him more pleasure than that relating to the propagation of Christianity among the natives." On October 15, 1816, Messrs. Poor and Warren took up their residence at Tellippalai, beginning on that day the work so long anticipated and so long to be continued, the preaching of the Gospel of Christ to the Tamils of Ceylon.

Interpreters were immediately available and regular preaching was undertaken at once. Thirty boys accepted an invitation to study under missionary supervision, the actual teaching to be done by native masters. The missionaries themselves went to work in earnest learning the Tamil language, with such success that Dr. Poor preached in Tamil just a year from the day he arrived in Tellippalai. Warren and Richards while not bearing the title of "doctor" had taken a year of medical study at the University of Pennsylvania and a year of practice in hospitals. Aided by Government officials and by private individuals they put up a small temporary hospital at Tellippalai and were able to relieve the sufferings of very many who came to them and who heard there for the first time the true story of the Physician of souls.

The very first letter from the Mission to the Prudential Committee urged the importance of sending more missionaries. When these four men found themselves face to face with Hinduism as they came to know it in Jaffna and realized that as the field was divided they were responsible for delivering the Good News to more than 50,000 people, people whose dire need of it was burned into their souls at every turn, they were appalled at the magnitude of the task. Their letters and journals are full of the cry of their hearts that God would send forth laborers into this harvest field and that He would bless them and make them efficient.

The people who from hearsay in Colombo had seemed so accessible proved on closer acquaintance to be strongly prejudiced against Christianity. Three hundred years before when conquered by the Portuguese the people had practically been forced into the Roman Catholic church, not wholly against their will for the new religion seemed to them to allow a sort of idolatry very like the old. But when the Dutch took possession in 1656 they earnestly set about converting the people to the Protestant faith. They destroyed the images of the saints, remodelled the churches to accommodate the whole population of the parishes and from time to time sent Chaplains to hold services. On such occasions peons were sent out to compel all the people to come in. Temples were torn down and multitudes of Hindus accepted baptism but carried on the worship of idols in inner rooms of their own houses. When the English in 1796 restored freedom of worship the people en masse reverted to heathenism. Their children had little love for the name or profession of Christianity. They were not personally hostile but they resented interference with the "custom of the country."

One wrote: "The aged will not and the young because of them dare not accept Christianity. They seem to have a settled determination to shield themselves from conviction. They almost fear lest they be so far instructed as to leave them without excuse." Appealing to American Christians for means to restore more of the ruined buildings offered for their use the missionaries wrote: "Every falling stone from these old churches mocks our delay and calls upon us to arise and wipe off the reproach cast on the Christian name."

RUINS OF PORTUGUESE CHURCH

Early the new Mission met the loss of one of their number who could ill be spared. Mr. Warren was suffering from tuberculosis even before they left America and Mr. Richards contracted the disease on the way out. Before they had been a year in Jaffna, in spite of all the measures suggested by the science of their day, it was found necessary to send them both on a voyage to the Cape of Good Hope where Mr. Warren died, Aug. 11, 1818. He was a peculiarly lovely and lovable Christian who did much to win friends for the

Mission everywhere. Mr. Poor was then stricken with the same disease, but later recovered. This was a time when remittances from America were slow in coming and the Mission suffered not only sorrow but actual want. Not from them but from English residents came the testimony; "Your missionaries are wearing out their lives by reason of hard labor and low living."

The Mission records of these days tell about a "monthly meeting" begun among all the missionaries of the Province, including now Wesleyan and Church Missions, where at the first meeting in August, 1819, the topic of the address was "Brotherly Love." This meeting has ever since been a delightful feature of missionary life in Jaffna, tending greatly to essential Christian unity. It was in December that year at the monthly meeting that a letter came stating that four new missionaries and their families had already reached Calcutta and were waiting for transport to Ceylon. The same day "while engaged in the interesting duties of the prayer meeting" records Dr. Poor, "we were interrupted by the arrival of another letter informing us that our brethren were actually in Ceylon, having landed at Trincomalee. On receipt of this information we were like them that dream." It would indeed be hard to overstate the joy that filled their hearts at the thought of these sorely needed helpers and at the assurance that God had not forsaken them. Dr. John Scudder and his wife started immediately, overland, to their relief, the rest of the party coming a few weeks later by boat. These were men and women destined to great service in the Mission field, aggregating nearly 250 years of labor, Rev. and Mrs. Levi Spaulding, Rev. and Mrs. Miron Winslow, Rev. and Mrs. Henry Woodward and Dr. and Mrs. John Scudder. They had had a great experience on the voyage out when the Spirit of God dealt with all in the ship till every seamen and every officer sought salvation. With splendid courage they came to their appointed work sure of God's presence and blessing.

It was natural that the Mission should pause at this time to take account of the work already done and in 1821 they made a formal review of the situation. In their five years occupancy they had established themselves firmly in the Jaffna district, occupying and carrying on evangelistic work in eight parishes. They had opened twenty-four free schools, employing of necessity Hindu teachers but keeping strict watch over the carrying out of their own plans. The children were all taught the truths of the Gospel and were habitual listeners to preaching on the Sabbath. At the stations where the missionaries lived they were training up a few of the more promising boys, wholly supporting them and keeping them constantly under the influence of the missionary home. Large numbers of Tamil men had heard the Gospel explained in street meetings, bazaar meetings, wayside preaching places and from house to house. A very few women had heard the truth but in general the homes of the people were yet unreached. Tracts both written and printed had been read by hundreds. A few hopeful conversions were seen among the boys long instructed or the people closely associated with the missionaries.

Among them three had been found who seemed fitted for the Christian ministry and they were licensed to preach the Gospel. Facing the facts as to idolatry and its influence on the lives around them the missionaries were often heavy hearted because the Cross was despised and its message rejected, yet they went on with their work, believing the promises of God.

In the first application to Government for authority to carry on the Mission, leave had been asked and granted to operate a printing press. There was a delay of several years in getting together the press and the supplies and the printer, but in 1820 the Board sent Mr. Jas. Garrett to take charge of this part of the work. To the astonishment of the Mission the Lieut-Gov. acting ordered him to leave the island at once, frankly stating that he considered it "an impertinence on the part of Americans to come to Ceylon for missionary work since every needed effort in that direction was already being made by his Majesty's Government." To this surprising change in official attitude a strong protest was made. It was supported by the Royal Chaplain, Mr. Twistleton, who referred the matter to England but to no avail. Mr. Garrett had to go. This brought up the plan, cherished from the beginning, of reaching out to the lost millions of India. There was now an opening on the mainland which the Jaffna brethren, in Dec. 1820, voted to enter, sending Mr. Garrett and two others of their number. Just at this time, however, came an urgent call for Mr. Garrett to join the Bombay Mission and it was decided to send him there but the other project was not given up. From this time until the personnel of the Ceylon Government changed and the official restrictions were removed was a period of very earnest, very strenuous work with far-reaching results.

GRAVE OF JAMES RICHARDS, TELLIPPALAI

In 1821 the Mission suffered the loss of Mrs. Susan Poor who went triumphantly Home after a life of loving service, the first of the devoted band who left little children motherless in a strange land. The whole Missionary Circle was drawn very closely together by this sad experience. The following year James Richards passed away. He had long been prevented by bodily weakness from taking an active part in the work of the Mission, very greatly to his sorrow and he grieved over his seemingly useless life. But he was mightly in prayer and counsel and his associates rejoiced at every added day of his fellowship. Richards was one of that memorable group of students at Williams College in 1806 who gathered under shelter of a haystack to pray for an open way to the regions beyond. In the providence of God he was the only one of them who ever served in the foreign field, and his six years were all years of illness and suffering. Yet he left a mark upon the work still uneffaced, and gave a service as valuable probably as that rendered by any other. The old monument in the Tellippalai compound commemorates James Richards and his obedience unto death.

II

1821–1833

"Showers of Blessing."

With the coming of substantial reinforcements the Mission began to plan largely and courageously for a permanent work. In 1820 Dr. John Scudder was licensed to preach, an event of great interest to the little Christian community and with his Tamil assistants he entered upon practical evangelism in connection with medical work.

In 1822 the boarding schools at the several stations had brought together a considerable number of young men, some of them open followers of Christ, who gave promise of great usefulness. Something must be done to provide for their future training if they were to be utilized in the work of evangelizing their own people. It was proposed to the Prudential Committee to undertake a Central School, "to be as much like a college in America as circumstances should permit." Seven striking reasons were outlined: 1, It would afford a means for the general diffusion of Christianity among the people; 2, It would strike at the very root of idolatry which is ignorance; 3, It would provide native assistants in all lines; 4, It would continue the education of boys already in school with economy of missionary time and strength; 5, It would stimulate the ambition of boys in the lower schools; 6, It would provide men effectively trained for the public service; 7, The facilities for such an enterprise were already at hand, including a sufficient missionary force, suitable native assistants and students prepared and waiting.

Acquainted with the seriousness of the need and with the possibilities of this undertaking it seemed to all the missionaries that it must meet immediate approval and they presented it with confidence to the Prudential Committee, to the Ceylon Government and to friends in England, America and the East. Some thousands of dollars were collected from independent sources before it became apparent that the Government would not allow the work to be carried on as first proposed. It was expressly stipulated that no more missionaries could join the force and no "College" could be established. Even under these limitations the Mission decided with the consent of the donors of the funds to go on with a "Central School" to provide for the education of the boys already on their hands. Nor did the American churches cordially support the plan though the Prudential Committee authorized its continuance and provided the funds. It was a far look from the immediate pressing needs of the Mission to the possibility of Christian leadership for a whole people and this statesmanlike vision was not granted to all.

The school opened July 22, 1823, under the charge of Dr. Poor. The first decision was to locate in Jaffna town, the natural center of the whole Province and negotiations were begun for the purchase of property there. This was reconsidered and a "temporary location" chosen at Vaddukoddai and the erection of suitable buildings provided for. Dr. Poor loved the direct preaching of the Gospel and undertook the new work only because of his profound

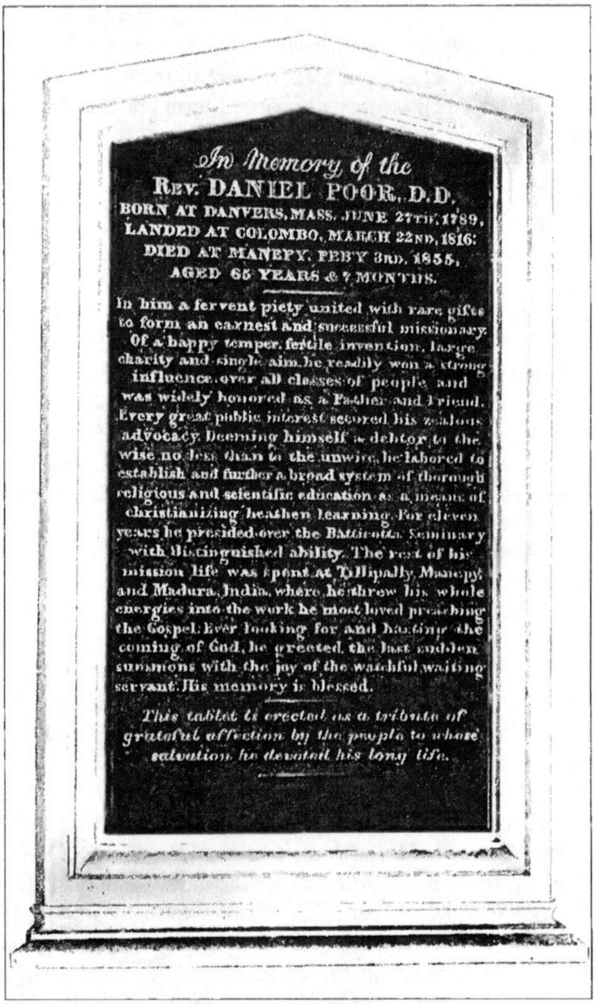

TABLET COMMEMORATING DR. POOR

conviction that it was the best way of dissipating error and disseminating truth, "preparing a people to receive the Gospel message and preparing men to give it."

Dr. Poor was no coward and stories are still told of how he demolished popular errors. Hearing that people said his students chose Christianity because of their ignorance of the Tamil sacred books he secured a copy of one of the Hindu Scriptures, the Canda Puranam held very sacred and read only by the priests in the temples and partially explained to the people there. This was read and interpreted into every-day Tamil in the presence of Dr. Poor's students. They were filled with confusion at hearing it thus contrasted with the pure and lofty precepts of the Bible and listened most respectfully to his appeal for honesty of thinking and chastity of life. There was also an interesting controversy with a Tamil pandaram about the time of an eclipse of the moon and its cause. Dr. Poor's calculations, thoroughly tested and agreeing with the Nautical Almanac proved exactly in accord with the movements of the heavenly bodies, greatly to the discomfiture of the people who had expected him to retreat in confusion.

Of far-reaching significance also was the opening of a Central School for girls at Uduvil under the charge of Mr. and Mrs. Winslow in 1824. Very gradually the prejudice against the education of girls had begun to break down. It was said when the missionaries went there that only two native Tamil women could read, aside from the dancing girls kept in the temples. The persistent kindness of the missionaries, aided by the special blessing of God, had won the confidence of the people so that in each station a few little girls were allowed to come to the veranda of the mission house for lessons.

The actual beginning at Uduvil was on this wise: one day two little girls were kept prisoners by a severe storm and cried for food and ate what Mrs. Winslow offered them. The next day their distracted father turned them over to her care saying that they had broken caste and he could not hope to provide for them in marriage. The missionaries gladly accepted the trust and took the girls under their charge, promising to educate and clothe and feed them free of expense to their parents, and to see that they were provided for matrimonially. Similar cases had come under the care of other missionaries and now, in 1824, the little girls from all the stations were brought to Uduvil to be under special instruction and care in one institution. Sir Richard Otley, then Chief Justice of Ceylon, and a warm friend to all missionary effort gave his encouragement to the Mission in the opening of this school, saying that "nothing could possibly help so to uplift a nation as the education and moral upbuilding of the mothers of generations to come." This was the first permanent boarding school on missionary soil and none has since surpassed it in the splendid quality of its service to the community and to the church. Thousands of girls have enjoyed its privileges and to a very large proportion of them it has proved to be the door of entrance to a Christian life.

By far the most striking thing in the history of the years under review is the series of revivals that began in 1824. In the last letter written by the Mission before their commencing these words occur: "Though the time should be far distant when the great harvest shall be gathered in IT WILL COME." At the last united prayer meeting in Dec. 1823, the presence of God was greatly felt and the missionaries, moved to confession and earnest pleading; were enabled to ask in faith for an outpouring of the Spirit. About the middle of the next month the boys in the boarding school at Tellippalai came to Mr. Woodward asking with tears what they should do to be saved. The following week similar scenes were enacted at Uduvil. The next day the monthly meeting was held at Vaddukoddai, "an occasion of Pentecostal power never to be forgotten?" At Panditerippu, a few days later, with no outward indication of unusual interest and during the absence of the missionaries, Amy, the negro girl who had worked in the Scudder family went to a Christian young man in the school and begged him to plead with the boys and invite them to come to Jesus and to warn them of their danger out of Christ. He said a few earnest words to them and left them. Soon a sound of crying arose, not from one but from many and when Dr. and Mrs. Scudder reached home they found the place filled with cries from one and another so long indifferent or hostile: "What shall I do?" "Have mercy, Jesus," "Forgive." Before he made any effort to quiet them Dr. Scudder knelt with his family and helpers to praise God. Then he rang the bell and the boys came in, many exhausted, many in tears. He sent them to their beds after a prayer together, and in the morning began the serious work of leading them one by one to the Rock of Ages. At Manepay and Vaddukoddai similar scenes were witnessed and large numbers of the young people under the care of the Mission found Christ.

PALMYRAH PALM AND CLIMBER

The hearts of the missionaries were greatly encouraged and after almost a year of testing and sifting out came a day of rejoicing when forty-one were added to the little church of thirty-seven members that had been eight years in gathering.

Later in the same year another wave of revival passed over the Mission showing itself at all the stations in fervent weeping prayer on the part of Christians and in deepened impressions on the hearts of those who had grown cold since the earlier one or who had been unwilling to yield then. At the close of 1825 also, the schools at Vaddukoddai and Tellippalai were swept with the winds of God's special grace, the boys from the latter school going to the Seminary to witness for Christ and to win new recruits for Him. Again at the close of 1826 the patient labors and earnest prayers of the Christians bore fruit in a new awakening among the unsaved and in a new love and zeal in their own lives. It must be remembered that a people so sunk in idolatry needed repeated rousing and warning before their repentance, in many cases, was genuine and thorough. This called for great patience, and faith on the part of the missionaries.

Many interesting experiences came to the Mission in these early years. The first women saved out of all the thousands around them were two girls who had been under the care of the missionaries at Tellippalai. One of them was shortly afterward married to a converted young man, this being the first Christian marriage celebrated. It was notable for the marked difference of caste, but the friends of both parties finally decided to attend the wedding and eat together on the Mission premises. Wonderful to the people was this little home, with its new standards of living, and where husband and wife actually ate together after asking God's blessing on the meal.

A circumstance that cheered the workers was an invitation from the wife of a village headman to hold a meeting for women in her house. Thus another long-closed door was opened. Even the Hindus seemed to recognize the truth of the Bible and contributed considerable sums to provide for its circulation. It was deeply touching to the missionaries to hear the court interpreter at Mallagam, himself a Hindu, read reverently from the Bible at a public meeting of the Bible association.

In one of his tours about the country, Mr. Poor crossed the "salt river" and entered a region where the truth had apparently never been preached except on one occasion by Dr. Scudder a few months previous. He found the native magistrate of Valvettiturai sitting in his veranda surrounded by sixty boys, his own charity school. His reception was most cordial and the manager offered to turn over the whole enterprise to the missionary if he would undertake it. It was pleasant to hear the boys recite the many Bible verses which Mr. Poor taught them and to see their interest in the new teacher they hoped to have. It was impossible at this time to take up the work, but this visit opened the way for permanent entrance into that field a few years later.

During this period the Mission had bitter experience of the ravages of cholera, when thousands of people were swept away. Among many others, one of the converts, Onesimus, was attacked by the disease and came to the missionary for medicine, insisting on taking time first for prayer and praise when time was very short. His recovery astonished the people, and still more did his peace of mind in the face of death and his singing the praises of God while suffering tortures from his sickness. The missionaries spent their strength without stint, longing to save lives and souls.

HINDU PROCESSION

Every sort of effort was put forth to win a hearing for the message. Besides preaching at the stations they branched out into special meetings in the villages preaching five or six weeks in a place, distributing tracts, speaking and praying with all the people and then passing on to a new village until the round of a large circle had been made. A new opportunity was found in the Pearl Fishery near Mannar where more than 100,000 people gathered for a few weeks, "seeking goodly pearls," a priceless opportunity for acquainting them with Jesus Christ. Bazaar preaching brought the truth to hundreds every week, sometimes under severe opposition. Voluntary preaching bands went out on Sunday afternoons to nearby villages. They visited the great temples at festival times to tell the people of a pure religion. Their hearts burned within them at the sight of gross idolatry and pitiful delusion, seeing men rolling over and over in the dust of the roads in fulfillment of vows and subjecting themselves to torture to appease the fancied anger of their gods. They were often hard used themselves but that they would have counted a little thing if they only could have seen the people turn from idols to serve the living God.

In 1830 the Mission premises at Manepay were destroyed by fire, Mr. Woodward and his family barely escaping with their lives. The Hindus rejoiced at this sign that their gods were awake and could make themselves felt. They were astonished to see the buildings repaired and occupied by two families instead of one. Friends of the Mission in Ceylon and India came so generously to the rescue that the damage was actually repaired before the American churches knew of the loss.

Under definite restriction as to the coming of more workers the men on the field felt they at least must do all they could do, for at best their years would be short for even beginning the task. New out-stations were opened and as fast as the increase in trained native helpers would warrant, the work was extended in all directions. There was sufficient increase in numbers by 1831 to justify the division of the one church into five which were to meet together for the quarterly communion and hold other services separately, sixty-nine members being enrolled at Vaddukoddai, forty-nine at Uduvil, twenty-nine at Tellippalai, twenty-four at Manepay, and twenty-one at Panditerippu.

A "Consociation" was formed at the same time, which continued until 1838 when it was changed to a "Presbytery." Formal instruction in theology was begun at the Seminary in addition to training a class of twenty helpers whom Mr. Winslow was already teaching at Uduvil. From time to time protracted meetings were held in the various stations nearly the whole missionary force being present and carrying on a diversity of meetings for Christians, for heathen and for inquirers, greatly to their own spiritual refreshment and to the increase of interest among the people. Mention should be made of the monthlys meeting long carried on by Mr. Woodward for the missionaries' own children, several of whom were there brought to Christ. They always remembered gratefully how he seized the opportunity to help them at just the time when they were ready for help. The mothers of these children had early

MANEPAY HOUSE IN 1916

formed a "maternal association" that met weekly to pray for and with the little ones.

At one or two stations "Christian congregations" were formed, the members declaring their belief in the Gospel and their purpose to renounce idolatry and all heathen ceremonies as well as to attend Christian worship. They did not count themselves personally as Christians but distinctly as being "on the Lord's side." They formed a hopeful field for instruction. At some stations special efforts were made to preach the Gospel to the very poor. The wretched pitiful beggars so common in the country were invited to come all at one time, usually on Sunday morning, and as they sat crouched on the veranda, 60 to 100 of them, their emaciation and rags bore testimony to the reality of their need. They were told the Old Story so new to them and were sent away happy with rice enough for a whole day of plenty.

The Seminary at Vaddukoddai was now well established and fully justified the hopes of its founders. Through its increasing success came the need for a combined preparatory Boarding School for boys and this was started at Tellippalai in 1825 and removed to Vaddukoddai in 1832. The small separate boarding schools however were not yet given up for they seemed to offer the best opportunity of all for really influencing life and character.

In 1830 all hearts rejoiced at the return of the Holy Spirit upon the Mission in reviving power. It began as before, in the meetings of the missionaries themselves after definite, believing, and united prayer. Then they went out with new courage to find their message accepted by the people who had opposed it. The influence was felt at all the stations, and more generally than in any former case. Special efforts were made to win the schoolmasters who had so long heard the truth, and some of them yielded to it this time. Sixty-one members were added to the church.

An open letter sent from the Mission some years earlier reads like a twentieth century document. It calls upon Christians everywhere to "make more marked distinction between the church and the world," urges "a close connection between all missionary societies" summons Christians to "perfect love" and to having more of Christ and less of self in all their plans, demands more system in planning and more energy in executing the work, "more gratitude to God and fewer thanks to living men," suggests a union world concert of prayer for Missions and a united deputation representing all Boards to visit all fields and report to the whole church.

One question which came up early in the minds of the missionaries and which was discussed at length in correspondence with the Board was that of the education of their own children. Several little ones had been given back to God by parents just as heartbroken as any in the homeland, but in 1830 there were fifteen children in the various missionary families. As they grew older the parents' hearts were torn between apparently conflicting duties. It was clear to them, knowing the conditions as those in America could not know them, that their children could not safely be brought up in Ceylon. No one had time to educate them separately without neglecting the legitimate work of the Mission. No conscientious parent would willingly place them under the contaminating influences of Hinduism so far as to have them in the native schools. And looking forward to their settlement in life they saw no way of honorable self-support for them in Ceylon. Wages, if they became common laborers, were only a few cents a day and they could not maintain American standards of living upon any wage possible to them there. In order to be of use as junior missionaries they would need the stimulating influences of a Christian education in a Christian land. The best interests of their health also demanded their removal to a colder climate. All these things, so obvious now, and to the minds of the parents so obvious then were repeatedly and earnestly set forth in letters to the Prudential Committee, who could not at once see in them any justification for the added expense involved. Finally permission was given to send the children home, if the parents would draw on their allowance to cover the passage money and provide privately for their support with personal friends. When Mr. Winslow, after the death of his gifted and devoted wife in 1833 proceeded to America with his three little girls other missionaries took the opportunity to send their children too. His landing in Boston with his little flock of eleven missionary children created great interest and brought vivedly to the minds of the friends there the one deep sorrow in the lives of missionaries, that of parting from their children for Christ's sake.

REV. MIRON WINSLOW

A little before this, Warren, the eight year-old son of Dr. Poor had been sent home with India missionaries returning. His (now) amusing accounts of missionary life, its "ease," its "extravagance" as it appeared to his horrified listeners, arising chiefly from a child's desire to impress his playmates with the charms of a life that seemed in retrospect so dear, aroused a storm of criticism. Reports of this coming back to Ceylon drew from the missionaries and especially from their wives particular and very instructive accounts of their manner of living. They showed the home church that the employment of servants for menial duties was not only justified but the only honest course when their own time, costing the churches perhaps $2.00 a day would accomplish no more than native servants could do at a cost of possibly 20 cents a day. The number of servants and their manner of work was for the first time explained so that it was seen that it was not from the choice of the missionary but from the necessity imposed by caste customs that so many were employed. There was a keen desire on the part of the Mission to have the matter thoroughly understood at home, for they were sure of approval if things were known just as they were and the reasons therefor.

Fifteen years had now passed since the work began and again the Mission paused to review the situation. They found that many children had been gathered into the Boarding Schools and had been savingly converted there. Thousands of other children had been instructed in the day schools and the Sabbath Schools and their minds stored with the fundamental truths of Christianity. Thousands of adults had been taught the Gospel by preaching and by visitation at their homes, a few of whom had given their allegiance to Jesus. They perceived a "silent but steady march of truth, the progress of minds awakened to think, the counter-currents beneath the still surface of heathenism, the effect of light on consciences not yet sufficiently alarmed to break out." The great mass of the people were still joined to their idols. "The vital need" they wrote, "is importuning prayer that God will rend the heavens and come down and cause the mountains to flow down at His presence."

III

1834–1842

"I will enlarge thy borders."

The welcome news was received in 1833 that the restrictions laid upon the Mission were removed and additions to the force might now be made. This followed upon the visit of the new Governor, Sir Robert Horton, who became greatly interested in the plans and progress of the Vaddukoddai Seminary. At once the Prudential Committee prepared to strengthen the Mission and during the year following sent out seven men and their wives and in 1835 three more. The coming of these recruits brought rejoicing to the Christians and some dismay to the Hindus who had been looking for the defeat of the whole enterprise.

It now proved possible to extend the work somewhat in Jaffna. New stations were opened at Varany and Chavakachcheri. Mr. and Mrs. Hutchings were added to the force at Vaddukoddai and after they had learned the language were sent for a time to the remote new station of Varany and then brought back to Uduvil and Manepay for their main work.

Mr. and Mrs. Minor took up the printing work at Manepay where the long-wished-for press was set up and with it the other press shipped out years before, lost in India, recovered and since loaned to the neighboring Church Mission at Nellore. Dr. and Mrs. Ward lived at Vaddukoddai to aid the Seminary force and develop medical work. Mr. and Mrs. Hoisington settled at Vaddukoddai where he became the head of the Seminary faculty and took the place of Dr. Poor when the latter removed to India. Mr. Hoisington proved to be of unusual scholarly tastes, and gifts, and his learning commanded respect among the people everywhere. His devotion to the Seminary was unbounded.

Mr. and Mrs. Apthorp, after some adjusting of appointments were sent to Varany to carve out of raw heathenism a church of the living God. They found it a place of difficulty as to climate and conditions but they were very happy in their work there, forming a little boarding school for girls which was greatly blest and establishing a small Christian colony. Mr. and Mrs. Perry had hardly more than begun the work in which they were so deeply interested when they were both stricken with cholera and died within a few days of each other.

The time had now come when the Mission could carry out its purpose of entering the white harvest fields of India. Several visits of inquiry had been made and Mr. Woodward, on a trip to the Nilgherry Hills just before his death at Coimbatore in 1834, secured formal permission from the Governor in Council to open missionary work in the Madras Presidency.

After long consideration the following assignments of workers were made.

To Madura: Rev. and Mrs. Todd, Rev. and Mrs. Lawrence, Rev. and Mrs. Hall, Rev. and Mrs. Eckard, and perhaps most important of all for the new undertaking, Dr. and Mrs. Poor, experienced and successful in the Tamil work. Three of the new missionary families therefore spent only a few months in Ceylon and thereafter appear in the records of the Madura Mission. Mr. and Mrs. Eckard were soon obliged to return to Jaffna for health reasons and were stationed at Vaddukoddai and later at Panditerippu. While at this station Mrs. Eckard opened the first "Infant School" in Ceylon modelled after the ones popular in America at that time. Mr. Eckard, a few years later counted it one of the most useful of his duties that he was then instructing all the native assistants except those at Chavakachcheri and Varany in Bible Study and theology.

In 1836 a second India Mission was opened at Madras with a view especially to the printing of Scriptures and tracts. Mr. and Mrs. Winslow lately returned from America and Dr. and Mrs. Scudder were set apart for this work. The Madras Mission was later taken over by the Dutch Reformed Churches of America — and thus in the providence of God the Ceylon Mission became the mother of the two great missions now known as the American Madura Mission and the American Arcot Mission.

The India work started also with efficient native Christian helpers, three of whom were sent over with Mr. Todd. They regarded themselves and were regarded by their friends as going to a very far country, for no one loves his home and his own village better than the Tamil. Ease of access soon removed this feeling and frequent visits strengthened the ties between the two mission. In 1837, however, the Uduvil school shared in a real foreign missionary enterprise by the marriage of one of the students to a Christian young man of the Church Mission, and their going to Penang, an island between Sumatra and Malacca, for definite Christian Service. This cost these young people as much by way of broken ties and worldly sacrifice as any missionary of the American Board has ever paid. A missionary society for carrying on Gospel work in and about Jaffna, "the Native Evangelical Society" had been organized in 1832, regularly employing catechists and teachers. Even before that, as early as 1827 there was a Tellippalai Christian School Society which supported an evangelist in the village of Erlalai and laid the foundations of the church to be founded there many years later. This was undoubtedly the first Home Missionary society formed in any foreign missionary field.

With the coming of so large a number of new missionaries it seemed as if the work must make rapid progress. In answer to importunate prayer a revival was felt in all the stations, in 1834, more searching and more permanent in effect than any yet experienced. A five days meeting at Vaddukoddai was followed by four days at Uduvil and Manepay with striking results, then a day of fasting and prayer, and later a joint meeting of 160 inquirers where the power of God was clearly seen. More than seventy were added to the Church this year, the largest number since the Mission began. The next year also was full of blessing and at its close revival fires were burning at all the stations. Great interest was aroused and some unfavorable comment as well as by Dr. Scudder's bringing to his new station at Chavakachcheri several of the girls of the Uduvil school to help in meetings for women and children by their songs and prayers and personal testimonies. These girls went with the missionaries to the day schools where they told the little Hindu children what Jesus had done for them and pled with them to seek the Lord. That the work was effective was shown by heathen parents being aroused to remove their children from the schools. The missionaries thanked God anew for the schools which gave them access to so many young hearts.

VILLAGE DAY SCHOOL

Again in 1836 Manepay and Uduvil were visited with revival not so far-reaching but bringing some few to repentance. The following year there was a season of marked religious interest at the seminary.

An interesting development during these years was the growth of temperance sentiment. The missionaries in 1830 were using wine and beer, as so many Christian people had done at the time they left America, believing them essential to health and not realizing how great a stumbling block they were laying in the path of the native church. When the reinforcement of 1834 came fresh from the temperance agitation in the United States none of them used alcoholic drinks, and their example together with the conviction already growing in the minds of the senior missionaries led to the abandonment of their use altogether. Dr. Scudder found his first temperance mass meeting so great a popular success as to convince him that the Mission ought to take a decided stand in the matter. A Jaffna Temperance Society was formed, uniting all factions in a common opposition to a common enemy.

The members of this third band of missionaries received quite differing impressions of the work they found in Jaffna. Some of them arraigned it seriously, deploring the want of Christian character among the people, seeing in the converts and native assistants little of honesty or purity or steadfastness and grieving over the wide social gulf fixed between the missionaries and the Tamil Christians. Others at the same time and with exactly the same facts before them expressed their wonder at the marvels God had wrought in making men so strong and so dependable out of such shifting, unchaste material. They rejoiced in the fact that the missionaries, though of the ruling race and color and necessarily regarded with some awe by the Tamils had so completely won their confidence, respect and love. All agreed that Christianity had made great

HINDU TEMPLE

progress in the country, thousands of people having heard its message of love and warning and being now within reach of its saving power.

In 1837 the Board found itself unable to continue supplies on so large a scale as before and retrenchment was ordered. The order was carried out, but at fearful cost, amid the open triumph of the Hindus and to the staggering of the faith of many Christians. The Seminary sent away forty-five students and refused to take the new class of forty. The native free schools were closed, catechists and teachers dismissed. One missionary wrote: "After my usual lessons with the readers in the schools yesterday I gave each one a portion of the Bible as a present. I told them the reason, exhorted them to read it, not to enter into temptation, to keep the Sabbath holy, prayed with them, commending them to the Friend of little children, and sent them away — away from me, from the Bible class, from the Sabbath School, from the house of prayer — to feed on the mountains of heathenism with the idols under green trees; a prey to the roaring lion, to evil demons, and to a people more ignorant than they, even to their blind, deluded and deluding guides — and when I looked after them as they went out, my heart failed me. O what an offering to Siva — five thousand children!" Closing up so large a part of the work developed through long years was like cutting off a hand or a foot to these men and women who had given their best to its upbuilding. It seemed an unmixed evil. Yet soon they found that they had needed the opportunity thus given to stop and inquire whether the plans they were following were really the best possible to them. They found the school work was overgrown, swallowing up time and funds needed for the symmetrical expansion of the whole work. The retrenchment, along with real hardship for many concerned and with injustice to some, furnished a needed test of sincerity and disinterestedness on the part of the Tamil helpers. It involved a sifting out very trying to all concerned but wholesome in its proof of loyalty in many and of failure in a few.

REV. AND. MRS. LEVI SPAULDING

Notwithstanding the gracious revivals of the 30's there now appeared a serious letting down throughout all the work. The confidence of the people in the Mission had been shaken by the retrenchment of 1837–9 and the missionaries themselves, physically weakened and sadly over-worked, gave away to the general depression and began to see disheartening difficulties. There were few accessions to the churches, the general spiritual state was low, and their hearts sank under the triple burden of material and spiritual and physical needs.

The work now made heavier demands through the opening of stations at Varanyand Chavakachcheri, in the development of the Seminary, in the operation of press; (and in the preparation of material for it) in the growth of the Uduvil school, in the increase of pastoral duties among the church members, and in the need for the better training of Tamil assistants. On the other hand the more experienced missionaries had been sent to India, only Mr. and Mrs. Meigs of the first group and Mrs. and Mr. Spaulding of the second group remaining. No others had been in the field long enough to be really free in the use of the language. An exceeding bitter cry of need came to the Board. Among all the needs mentioned above they felt chiefly the need for "men adapted to thorough patient pastoral work among the people, in order even to hold the ground already occupied as well as to bring the Gospel to bear on the thousands yet untouched." Some of the force were invalided home. Mr. and Mrs. Meigs went to America on account of their family. Blow after blow fell upon the weakened Mission until it came near to real disheartening.

In the long interval before men could be sent from America the Madura Mission came to the rescue, sending Mr. and Mrs. Cope to the Seminary at Vaddukoddai and Dr. and Mrs. Poor for evangelistic work at their old station at Tellippalai. This put new heart into the over-burdened and almost worn out force of workers.

Mr. Meigs returning from America in 1842, and leaving his family there brought three new missionaries and their wives, J. C. Smith, Samuel Whittlesey and Robert Wyman. Mrs. Smith was seriously ill during the voyage and died within a month after reaching Jaffna. The other young people had been earnestly at work on the language during the voyage and were soon able to be of great assistance. Mr. Wyman's health failed after only a year or two of work and he died on the voyage home undertaken in the hope of prolonging his life. Mr. and Mrs. Whittlesey were moved from station to station as the work demanded saving at one point or another even if lives should be sacrificed in the process. They were stationed at Manepay and then at Chavakachcheri where they longed to stay and see the work grow to real success, and then were sent to Uduvil to take charge of the Girls' Boarding School, while the Spauldings went to America after twenty five years of continuous service. Mr. Whittlesey died in India in 1847 and his wife then returned to America.

Some years before the suggestion had come from one of the missionaries returning from America that possibly "unmarried females" might come to conduct infant schools and to supplement the efforts of the missionary wives which were so circumscribed by their domestic duties. This revolutionary idea was thoroughly discussed, and it was the consensus of opinion that the single woman would be very useful indeed in the missionary work but an unknown quantity in the missionary family. There the matter rested until the pressure of the need for workers grew unbearable and then the request was made that the Board endeavor to find young women who should — the record hints — combine all the virtues which experience had shown to be desirable in missionary wives.

In response to this appeal three young women were sent out, one of them accepting the invitation of Rev. Mr. Cherry to join the Madura Mission as his wife almost before she had set foot in Ceylon, one of them, Miss Brown, returning to America on account of ill health next year, while the third, Miss Eliza Agnew, entered upon her marvelous career of forty years in connection with the Uduvil school for girls.

MISS ELIZA AGNEW

Added to the scarcity of funds and the lack of laborers was the far severer trial of discipline in the native church. Some prominent mission assistants had fallen under censure for making heathen marriages and for other complicity in Hindu practices. In view of these abuses it was resolved in 1841 to deal directly and decisively with the native ministry on the following points: 1, the support of caste; 2, covetousness; 3, the use of "sacred ashes"; 4, the lack of brotherly love; 5, neglect of work and study; 6, false standards of living; 7, personal influence for heathenism. A day of humiliation and prayer was appointed and deeply conscious of the seriousness of the situation the missionaries and the native preachers met to consider all these points. It was decided to suspend all four of the preachers from their office, two of them afterward being restored after ample confession and promise of amendment.

Hardly had this trial passed when one even more overwhelming came upon the Mission. It came to the ears of the Seminary faculty that some of the pupils had been away at night attending heathen dances and rites at Araly, a village near. In the course of a quiet investigation they found a large number of boys and several teachers involved. Probing deeper they uncovered a shocking condition of immorality practiced by nearly all the pupils and by some of the masters. This had without doubt long been known among the people at large to whom it would not appear very improper as long as it was concealed. The whole Junior class was dismissed and such other students as appeared to be contaminated with vice. This created a great stir and many complaints were heard but undoubtedly it did more to establish the real meaning of the Christian teaching about purity and truth than a hundred years of proclaiming it would have done.

The statement at the close of 1843 declared: "We have taken many outposts and some strongholds and from the heights that we have reached we may leisurely survey the extensive dominions of the adversary believing that what we have hitherto done is only preparatory to the final subjection of the whole ot our Lord.

1. Our hearts are set on the spiritual prosperity and the final salvation of the 460 church members now living.

2. We have not done with the 62 persons who have been excommunicated. Our hope is that some Peters among them, though now living in denial of their

Lord, will receive a look or a rebuke from Him that will melt their hearts and bring them back.

3. The young men educated in our Boarding Schools are mostly convinced of the truth. Their accession to the Church would double its size and extend its influence.

4. The tens of thousands, of both sexes, instructed in the principles of Christianity in the village schools, are many of them waiting for a change of times when they will feel at liberty to act on the light they have received.

5. We have access to the people. We are understood. The precious seed is sown. But laborers cannot produce a crop. May the Lord of the harvest cause the dews of heaven to descend and the floods to be poured out.

6. However feeble this is a branch of that church against which the gates of Hell cannot prevail."

IV
1846–1854

"Bearing Precious Seed."

During the years from 1846 to 1854 the personnel of the Mission was constantly changing. Mr. and Mrs. Mills came in 1849, but they were never well, and to their deep sorrow were forced to give up the struggle for health and return to America. During their brief connection with the College occurred another of those precious seasons of revival more familiar a dozen or more years before.

Mr. and Mrs. Noyes were three years in the Mission before being transferred to Madura — Mr. and Mrs. Lord served for a brief period and then joined the Madura Mission — Mr. and Mrs. Burnell took up the work long carried on by the Minors at Manepay and carried it until plans were changed and the Mission was no longer in a position to have a printing establishment. The return of Wm. W. Scudder in 1847 to the land of his birth and boyhood was of deepest interest to the Tamil people. They sorrowed with him in the loss of his young wife who died from cholera, and regretted his going to America after a few years with his motherless child and his later decision to work in India rather than in Ceylon.

In view of these many changes the "labors abundant" of the three oldest missionaries of the field, Meigs, Poor and Spaulding were a constant surprise to the friends of the work. It was they who were able by their greater knowledge of Tamil to preach freely and frequently and it was their delight to do so. On the occasion of the thirtieth anniversary of his arrival there Dr. Poor arranged and carried out a striking series of meetings designed to arrest the attention of the whole district. Quite in accord with Tamil thinking he proposed a series of collections from all who had shared in the benefits of the Mission, and used these funds to help the Christians in several villages to erect houses of worship there. Father and Mother Spaulding returned from their one furlough earnest and vigorous, ready for another quarter century of service. Mr. Meigs, living alone, with his wife and children still in America, did an amazing amount of work and all of them as they ripened and mellowed in longer fellowship with Christ were increasingly useful. Meanwhile the younger men were working in, but several of them stayed only a few years and were never equipped to do efficient Tamil work. There were some happy exceptions to this general rule, among those who joined the staff in the 40's, notably Mr. and Mrs. Howland, Mr. and Mrs. Hastings, Mr. and Mrs. Smith, and Dr. Green. The constant changes however kept the Mission always short handed and the records give an impressive picture of the little group who went quietly on in the midst of staggering disabilities as to health and numbers, trusting

God, working hard and loving the brethren in the Mission and in the native church.

The whole question of the policy of the Mission was kept constantly agitated from America. The patrons of the Board were disappointed in not receiving reports of greater accessions to the church and they were forever asking "Why"? Indeed the missionaries asked the same questions with great searching of heart. They wrote in answer to inquiries from the Board full and instructive statements regarding certain features of the work. The whole matter of the need for and value of a native ministry was discussed at length, the Mission, in 1847, not believing it then needed or available or desirable. This view was modified within a few years.

Criticism kept coming on the score of the school work and the Mission were forced to think through their reasons for the policy they pursued. To these criticisms one of the Tamil assistants made the following striking reply: "I called a carpenter to make a door and he brought his adze and plane and other tools. I rebuked him saying, 'I told you to make a door. I did not tell you to bring an adze or a plane or to work with them.'" Whatever the outcome and whatever the personal love of some of the missionaries for direct evangelistic work they came out of the fiery trials of these years firmly committed, for better, for worse, to the policy of the school and the printed page as God's chosen implements in their hands for evangelizing the Tamils of Ceylon.

The vexed question of "caste" was thoroughly discussed, and each missionary and several of the catechists wrote full and frank statements for the information of the home churches. Agitation of this subject began early. A resolution regarding it appeared on the record of July 1823, when it was decided that no distinction of caste could be tolerated in the new Seminary at Vaddukoddai. The following year it was declared: "We know no distinction of caste at the Lord's table." Often thereafter the matter came up. This subject as it is in Jaffna has never been and is not today rightly understood because of the inevitable tendency to draw analogies from India where the conditions are absolutely different. At this time it was pointed out that by taking the communion together, by allowing their sons and daughters to live together with children of other castes in the Boarding Schools, by their own eating and drinking with other Christians of all castes and by their eating food prepared and served by low-caste cooks in the Mission houses and by numerous other practices the Christians from high-caste families had done enough to break their caste a hundred times over. The peculiarity of the case in Jaffna is that because of the good social position of many of the early converts it is no disgrace to be a Christian and the Hindus usually insist upon keeping up friendly relations. This involves a thousand difficulties, all tending to confuse the conscience and break down real piety. It is almost impossible for the most rigid opponent of caste observance to say where Christian courtesy ends and compromise begins. The missionaries did not hesitate to declare the whole counsel of God regarding real brotherly love and to legislate and discipline where need arose but their hope was in the sanctifying influences of God's spirit in the hearts of the Christians rather than in rules, however strict and however strictly enforced. They were not entirely agreed as to the wisest course but the majority resolved in 1848 to "increase effort to eradicate the caste spirit, using as weapons the light and love of the Gospel."

A great achievement and a great gift to the Tamil people was the publication of a Tamil Dictionary. This had been begun by Rev. Mr. Knight of the church Mission and was carried to completion by Mr. Spaulding with learned native assistance. About the same time an English-Tamil dictionary begun by Mr. Knight came into Mr. Spaulding's hands for completion and later was turned over, practically finished, to Mr. Samuel Hutchings then of the Madras Mission for final revision. Rev. Miron Winslow formerly of the Ceylon Mission compiled a Tamil-English dictionary, starting with manuscripts prepared by Mr. Knight but going on to complete an authoritative lexicon remarkably full and accurate. All these were printed on the American Mission Press at Madras and have been invaluable to English and American students of Tamil and to Tamil students of English.

For many years the missionaries tried faithfully to stay by the work in Ceylon asking neither furlough nor release until absolutely incapacitated for further labor. Finally a new policy was adopted, that of taking regular seasons for rest and recuperation before health should fail. A house was built upon the Palani Hills within the Madura field for their residence, a measure well planned to save the needless waste of precious lives. Reinforcements came too slowly, however to save the situation and there is no doubt that health and lives were sacrificed and progress in the work was hindered by the failure of the church to meet the need in time. Mr. Hoisington, returning far too soon for his own good in 1845, spoke of the "labor and care-worn forms of the missionaries" and although he knew he was shortening his own life by it, rejoiced "to have come at such a time as this."

In 1845-6 occurred the most fearful scourge of cholera ever known in Ceylon. It was estimated that one-tenth of the population was swept away. Ordinary missionary operations gave place largely to ministering to the sick and bereaved. The people flocked to the temples and beggared themselves, but were afraid to take the medicines offered by the Government and the Missions.

Again in 1846 the Mission was cheered by the coming of Rev. Wm. W. Howland and his wife, and Rev. and Mrs. A. H. Fletcher, the latter to stay less than four years and the former more than forty. Mr. Fletcher was one whom the special needs of the work sent to station after station, Manepay and Tellippalai and Chavakachcheri and Varany all in little more than three years. The Howlands, assigned to Vaddukoddai, greatly strengthened the "station work," training native assistants and directly preaching the Gospel and overseeing schools. Mr. Howland's humble spirit rejoiced in all the signs of progress among the people, and was willing always to decrease that they might increase.

In 1847 a serious attempt was made to replace with Christians all the Hindu schoolmasters connected with Vaddukoddai station. This was a long step in advance and while it caused hard feeling among the Hindus it was generally recognized as just. More emphasis was placed, throughout the Mission, on the girls' schools, by giving the masters a little larger wage for maintaining their attendance and special prizes to the girls themselves. The Ceylon Government offered to co-operate in this work and it was voted to "allow them to pay the expenses of twenty-five girls in the Uduvil and Varany Schools." One of the village schools for girls was named "Barley Wood" in recognition of a donation received from Miss Hannah Moore, thus linking the education of girls in Ceylon with the educational work of that great English philanthropist and author.

URICARDU BUNGALOW

In 1846 the Mission voted to put the Boarding School at Uduvil under the charge of two single ladies responsible to a committee of the Mission. It is difficult at this distance of time to estimate the revolutionary character of this action. To be sure the business management was kept in the hands of a committee of which the resident missionary was chairman, but the internal arrangements of the school were turned over to Miss Agnew and Miss Capell. For a time they were assisted by Mrs. Apthorpe who had remained in the work after her husband's death in the new Mission bungalow at Uricardu at the time when the field was being opened for the Udupiddi work in 1844.

In 1850 after several very interesting conversions in the Vaddukoddai Seminary a real revival of unusual power was felt. This deeply affected the Christians leading them to self-examination, to confession and to a new union with Christ. The unsaved, many of whom had long resisted the truth, were convicted of sin, made thorough repentance and were as happy in the realization of the Saviour's love as any converted in Christian lands.

V

1855–1865

"They shall not labor in vain."

In 1855 the Prudential Committee sent its Senior Secretary, Dr. Rufus Anderson, and Rev. G. C. Thompson, a pastor who was also a member of the Committee to visit the India Missions "with full power and authority to give such directions as they judged the best interests of the Missions should demand, their action to be subject to the revision of the Prudential Committee and ultimately to that of the American Board." In the Ceylon Mission younger men had come in who saw things differently from the time-honored veterans and there had arisen differences of opinion as to the best interests of the work. It has been the glory of this Mission that such differences have often existed without prejudice to the Christian fellowship of those who differed. Father Spaulding put it clearly: "If I find I cannot bring my brethren to my way of thinking it remains for me to bring myself to their way of thinking and so preserve the unity of the Spirit in the bonds of peace." It was something of a relief to have the matters in which there was honest difference of opinion together with others in which there was practical unanimity brought out into light for thorough discussion and for decision.

After reading the whole procedure of the Deputation given in the written notes from day to day, in the printed reports, in the Mission records of the meetings, and the full correspondence, it is impossible to escape the conclusion that the Deputation went to India with opinions already formed and with plans already formulated for the action of the Missions. However, in Ceylon they spent two months in patient and thorough investigation, then assigned each subject of inquiry to a committee of missionaries whose findings were freely discussed and revised by the whole Mission in conference with the Deputation. Certain conclusions were arrived at of far-reaching importance. These conclusions were judged by the majority to be the best under the circumstances and they expected to stand by them. Some expressions of dissatisfaction however crept into their private letters home which were widely quoted in America and aroused a storm of opposition to the adoption of any report embodying the changes proposed. The subject was referred to a special meeting of the American Board called for its consideration at Albany after the return of the Deputation and thence, after long discussion, to a special committee of thirteen who were instructed to report to the Board at its regular meeting in Oct. 1856. Full opportunity was given every missionary in the three India fields to state his whole opinion in the matter and after careful consideration of all the correspondence and reports the committee found that the changes were justified by the conditions and that nothing could be gained by reversing them. The Board accepted this report and the Mission proceeded as best it could to carry out the recommendations.

Briefly they were these: English education was abolished *in toto*. The Vaddukoddai Seminary and the station English schools were summarily closed and all English was eliminated from the course of study at Uduvil.

2. The number of pupils at Uduvil was reduced to twenty-five, the number estimated as "needed for wives of the Christian helpers in the Mission."

3. A maximum wage for helpers was set, somewhat lower than the highest then paid.

4. Government grants-in-aid of the schools were declined and the number of schools reduced.

5. Separate churches were established and native pastors ordained and set over them.

6. The Mission Press was passed over to native management.

The first of these changes cut the deepest. In Ceylon, then, as now, English was the official language, the requisite for all public service, the language of all proper ambition on the part of Tamil youth. They sought it, doubtless, with a view rather to financial and social self-improvement than to Christian service, but this is true in all countries. One thing was certain. The leaders of the Ceylon people would be educated in English by some agency and it was for the Mission to say whether this agency should be Christian or not. Strangely enough it was the older members of the Mission who saw this clearly and who were forced to yield to others less far-sighted. The closing of the Seminary would have been the more regretted by the Mission had there been any practical way of keeping it open, but with the cutting down of the force and the added burdens laid upon men already ill it was almost a relief to have the Seminary out of the way. The thing that had caused most dissatisfaction with its work was the fact that comparatively few staunch and earnest Christians came from its doors. Yet after the lapse of years how they stand out, those leaders in church and community whose training was received in the Old Seminary.

Uduvil had done a great work in training Christian mothers for a new generation. In the first forty years of the Mission 394 girls had been received of whom 344 had graduated or left to be married, nearly all having married Christians. Of their children 550 had already been baptised and were under Christian care. They were found in every walk of life, always exerting a great influence for good, "the most pleasing result of labor to be seen in the Mission — but the life boat is not full," wrote one who mourned the missing of the great opportunity. The attempt was made in all honesty to cut down the numbers to "those needed as helpers in our own field." However, God's plans were not to be thwarted by a temporary misunderstanding of them and the school within a few years resumed its place as the leading institution in all Jaffna for educating young women and for winning them to Christ.

The inevitable result of setting a wage scale and setting it low was twofold:

TAMIL PASTORS IN 1898

BIBLE WOMEN IN 1910

the larger part of the men well qualified as helpers went to other fields in mission or government employ thus crippling the local work seriously; the few who stayed by the mission proved their faithfulness and found a real reward in added confidence and responsibility. The rise of wages due to increased cost of living and higher standards of living was only briefly deferred.

Time fully vindicated the action taken with relation to the Tamil pastorate. Interest and devotion and self-sacrifice were certainly stimulated by the ordination of these men who were to be supported mainly by their own churches, first Rev. M. Cornelius at Karadive, then Rev. D. Stickney at Valanai. Another effort was made at this time to stamp out caste from the churches, by the signing of a solemn covenant by nearly all the leading Christian men who affirmed their own purpose to be free from caste and to purify the church and who sealed the covenant with a love feast, eating food prepared in defiance of caste rules by low caste cooks. No one seems then to have seen that the stronghold of caste is in family relations and that this action needed the co-operation of the Christian women to make it effective.

The program for a meeting of the Tamil and foreign pastors in 1858 shows how seriously they regarded their responsibilities and how like these were to those of pastors in the home churches.

1. "As pastors and leaders of God's people, what does our office and what does He that gave it require of us?" — *Rev. M. D. Sanders.*

2. What are the causes of the prevailing indifference in the churches?" —*Rev. M. Cornelius.*

3. "In what condition should a church be to be sure of the special favor of God?" — *Rev. T. P. Hunt.*

4. "What means does the Lord require of us to insure this condition?"— *Rev. E. P. Hastings.*

5. "Shall we be free from the blood of souls if we fail to use these means?" — *Rev. L. Spaulding.*

The Mission press had printed during the twenty years of its operation some 172 million pages of Christian literature and had exerted a strong influence in India as well as in Ceylon. It fell under the Deputation pruning knife in 1855 and part of it was sold and part of it was leased to a firm of Tamil Christians who had learned the business, the Mission proposing to pay them for such work as they proved to be competent to do. This was never wholly satisfactory as the equipment was not kept up nor the standard of work maintained. In 1866 Mr. Hunt, an American printer from the Madras Mission, made a careful inspection of the plant and on his recommendation the Mission furnished funds for a new native firm, Strong and Asbury, to buy out the interest of the retiring partner and to secure proper type to do good printing. Four years later the Mission again came to the rescue, turning over to the firm the publication of the "Morning Star" on condition that a full column of religious matter be printed each time and that the high moral standard of the paper be maintained. The Mission subsidized the undertaking to a limited extent and turned over half of the subscriptions, advertising and collections of that year, the firm to be responsible thereafter. They also gave the free use of the Mission premises for the work. The "Morning Star" founded in 1840 has exerted a powerful influence on public opinion in Ceylon, usually under the editorship of some member of the Mission, and printed in both English and Tamil. In 1859 Messrs. Sanders and Hitchcock were directed to begin the issue of a children's paper the "Paliar Nasan" which continued many years a valuable medium of religious instruction.

Some outstanding benefits appear from the visit of the Deputation of 1855. The pouring in of men and money with little local co-operation gave place to a gradual development of local resources. The native church was established on a firm basis with a pastorate raised up among the people and in part responsible to them. The schooling so long furnished free the people found they could themselves support. Undoubtedly the Christians of the Ceylon Mission had been made too dependent on foreign help. Now they were perhaps too suddenly thrown into the waves to sink or swim. With some struggling and strangling they swam.

The years immediately following these changes were hard years, not only because of the overturning of plans long cherished and the introduction of methods yet untried but because of the failure of the Board to send reinforcements in time. Nine missionaries and seven wives and one single woman comprised the active force in 1855. Only two years later four of the whole number had gone to America, six were invalids seeking health at Sanataria, one family had been transferred to Madura, leaving only three ordained men in the field, of whom one had been at work almost forty years. At one time the force was reduced to one man and two women, yet broken and beaten and cast down they refused to be defeated and held on in faith looking to God for help.

The depression in the Mission from overwork and discouragement is reflected in the history of the church during this period. There were occasional evidences that God had not forsaken His people but there was no in-gathering such as was longed for. For fifteen years continued this hard period of repression and depression. The plans made at the time of this Deputation were made conscientiously and with a sincere desire to promote the first and main objects of the Mission, the winning of the people to Christ and building them up in Christian character. As time went on it became apparent, however, that the changes had been too drastic and many plans were modified while some were reversed altogether.

None of the Deputation and few of the missionaries imagined that there would be any serious difficulty in effecting the change from English to vernacular education. They thought that firmness in recommending it, kindness in urging it and efficiency in providing it would be enough. As a matter of fact the change never was made as contemplated in 1855, the Tamil Christians with patience and yet with great persistence holding to their purpose to educate at least their own children as they had begun.

To be sure Vaddukoddai Seminary was closed and a Tamil Training and Theological Institution took its place. The latter was designed to "supply Christian workers not too highly educated to be useful among the humblest but rooted and grounded in Biblical truth and fitted to impart it." It accomplished a good work and one long needed in addition to that of the Seminary and it turned out some great men who did great things for God. Yet it was never to any considerable extent a substitute for the older institution. The Mission could not give attention enough to make it as great a success as had been hoped. The labor and expense of translating English textbooks into Tamil was never fully met. It had to depend largely for its scholastic success and often for its very continuance on the Seminary it was intended to supplant.

After the closing of the English schools at the various stations Tamil Christians came forward to teach such schools themselves, paid by the tuition and later, after their stability had been tested, by the Government grants-in-aid. Hindu English schools also sprang up. Even the schools nominally Christian were not under systematic religious instruction and of course were not under Mission supervision. Regular visits and Bible teaching by the missionaries would have been welcomed but their hands were far too full with other and often less fruitful labors.

The village vernacular schools were cut down and the years just following were a constant struggle to keep their numbers down. The people had been taught to desire education and now they would have it. In general they sent the children for a few years only to the vernacular schools, passing them on to private English schools as soon as they could afford it. No longer in the place of commanding influence but "now become the tail and not the head" the American Mission worked away at its problem of Christian education. Nowhere was the policy of exclusion less satisfactory than in the case of the girls. Cutting off the rewards for attendance discouraged the teachers and cutting off the hope of entering Uduvil discouraged the girls themselves. Some girls' schools were begun by the Tamil Christians, most of them later coming under the care of the Mission and being carried on, ultimately by foregn funds. Father Spaulding kept before the Board and so far as he could reach it, before the public a defence of the school systems untimely cut off. He vigorously denounced the new policy and the last heart-broken plea of his old age was on behalf of the thousands of Hindus unreached and out of reach. He lived to see the inevitable reaction, the tardy yielding to pressure of circumstances what he had always advocated as essentially Christian and right and wise but a generation of Tamil youth had meanwhile passed forever out of the reach of Christian instruction in their formative years.

The effort to establish native churches under pastors of their own went on slowly, as all things do in Jaffna, but with marked success. The first separate church, in Karadive, constituted at the time of the Deputation's visit, prospered for some years under the care of the pastor ordained at that time, but later this work became less fruitful and he was transferred to another field and finally dismissed from the ministry altogether. Rev. T. P. Hunt, ordained pastor over the church at Chavakachcheri, proved to be a man of ability who served many years usefully and acceptably. The Christians of Navaly, set off into a separate church in 1860 and given a pastor of their own in Rev. Francis Asbury were led and blest and prospered by God. So also the ordination of Rev. B. H. Rice at Vaddukcddai at the beginning of a pastorate of thirty-eight years, was an occasion of great rejoicing to the church and the Mission. Rev. D. Stickney had already been ordained and put in charge of a congregation. The missionaries, always conscientious, hesitated long before recommending these steps but the event richly justified their wisdom. These pastors were good men, sincere lovers of their Lord and acquainted with Him in daily fellowship. They were not always wise nor always right but they were taught and led by God. On the whole their ordination was a matter of sincere rejoicing to the whole Mission.

With every department of the work crying for reform and advance the Mission found its most serious problem in the steady depletion of the force. There were times when it was seriously considered both in America and in Ceylon whether it were not better to withdraw and leave the field to English societies. Some of the Mission begged that this might be done outright rather than that they should be left to struggle with burdens five times what they could hope to bear. Rev. Jas. Bates on the field only two and a half short years and then sent home supposedly to die, wrote fifty years later with bitter remembrance of what it meant under these conditions of need, to be told to "retrench." Where should it be? The missionaries began with their own salaries, and cut them as the event proved, to a point below the possibility of getting through without debt. Then they considered the pastors, with salaries already less than a third of what their ability and training would command elsewhere. These could not be reduced. On catechists, cutting a few cents here, and a Rupee there, they saved a little. The hardest of all was closing the schools. Yet it must be done. This was remembered as their "hardest day's work on the field."

The medical work begun by Richards and Warren at Tellippalai in 1816 and continued by Dr. John Scudder at Panditerippu and Chavakachcheri, came under the care of Dr. Nathan Ward in 1834 when the opening of the India work took the Scudders to Madras. Dr. Scudder was essentially an evangelist and gave the evangelistic impulse to his assistants in the medical work. Practical medical training was begun by him in 1832. The little hospital which he erected still stands at Panditerippu and is now used for a pastor's study Dr. Ward was a teacher as well as a physician, living at Vaddukoddai and sharing in the work of the Seminary. Rooms for the care of patients were fitted up for him in the Mission buildings there in 1841. Some eight or ten men were trained in medicine and each of the principal stations had its own native physician or

DR. SCUDDER'S FIRST HOSPITAL, NOW A PASTOR'S STUDY AT PANDITERIPPU

dispenser under Mission employ. Dr. Ward returned to America in 1847 and fourteen years later when the Mission was again without a physician he offered to fill the gap but died on the voyage out and was buried at sea.

Dr. Samuel Fisk Green, the out-standing Tamil Medical Missionary of his day, came to Jaffna in 1847, "first, to be physician to the missionaries and then to be of use to the heathen round about." After a few months at Vaddukoddai where he used the equipment and continued the work of Dr. Ward he removed to Manepay and commenced a work destined to grow to large proportions and to exert wide influence. At once he began training Tamil young men who should do, he hoped, far more than he could do directly to "raise the whole standard of medical practice among the Tamils, substituting science for superstition and honorable practice for quackery."

DR. SAMUEL FISK GREEN

Dr. Green's first classes were instructed in English but he soon found that the English terms in medical textbooks were practically unintelligible even to educated Tamils. The task of accurately defining in Tamil the terms used was immediately undertaken, rather the creation of a medical nomenclature in the Tamil language, a stupendous task which occupied many years. Along with this Dr. Green undertook the translation of textbooks as needed by his classes. A standard textbook was selected and a chapter translated with the aid of a munshi. This translation was dictated to the class with explanations and enlargement as needed to render it thoroughly understood. They transcribed it and then their copies were carefully compared with Dr. Green's, corrected and revised and a fair copy made. This laborious process went on for years. Additional translators and munshis and copyists were employed and finally Dr. Green succeeded in getting through the press the following books, some 4000 pages in all: Cutter's Anatomy, Physiology and Hygiene, Maunsell's Obstetrics, Druitt's Surgery, Gray's Anatomy, Hooper's Physician's Vade Mecum, Well's Chemistry, Dalton's Physiology, Waring's Indian Pharmacopoeia. Several of these bore the name of the Tamil physicians trained by Dr. Green, his loyal assistants in the work. In addition to these translations valuable vocabularies were printed which were accepted as authoritative in India as well as in Ceylon. Many popular treatises and tracts were issued which brought scientific truth to the people at large. Dr. Green's peculiarly good use of the Tamil language, free and idiomatic, was partly owing to a weakness of the eyes in the earlier years which kept him from prolonged book study and sent him out among the people to learn their speech.

It was Dr. Green's ambition to train one native physician for each 10,000 of the population, some thirty five in all and to see them settled in their own villages, independent practitioners, taking the place of the old Tamil hereditary doctors. As a matter of fact he trained about sixty, half of them in the vernacular and half in English. They were in demand for Government positions

DR. GREEN'S FIRST HOSPITAL, NOW THE MEN'S WARD AT MANEPAY

and were sent to various parts of the Island. Some settled as he had planned, in the immediate field of the Mission and the aim of making the medical graduates useful to their own people was secured to a good degree.

Dr. Green was a pioneer in proposing to make the Medical department gradually self-supporting by getting the people to pay something for medicines and treatment, a fair charge for both these being far below what they were accustomed to pay for native treatment. He succeeded in collecting some such fees but not extensively. The Government officials had confidence in Dr. Green's methods for they gave him an annual grant, £50 at first, then of £100 and later of £200 and continued this for ten years after his departure and until it was definitely decided by the American Board to send no foreign physician in his place. He was invited to take charge of the Friend-in-Need Hospital in Jaffna town, and did so for five years at great cost of labor to himself because of the opportunity it gave him to preach the Gospel to 8000 more people every year and because of the benefit to his students from seeing so large a number of cases.

Dr. Green made it his practice to commend Jesus Christ to every patient and to ask the help of God in the presence of his students at every operation. He was in earnest in believing that the medical work could and should contribute to the evangelization of the country and he labored zealously for and with his own students to that end. Ten years he spent in Jaffna, then after an interval of five years at home, he married and returned for a second ten years, and would gladly have returned for a third term of service had not the Board then adopted a policy of cutting down the medical work in all its Missions, a policy afterwards happily reversed but too late to save Dr. Green to Ceylon.

After he left the Island two classes in medicine were instructed by his students before the Government undertook the work in English at Colombo.

Twice at least during Dr. Green's years in Ceylon there occurred a fearful epidemic of cholera which he was helpful in combatting. He took the disease in 1855 just after the death from cholera of good old Dr. Poor, and on his recovery gave himself to the cure and prevention of cholera in the province. In 1866 again there were many thousands swept away by this disease, the native church suffering grievous loss. The whole Mission devoted itself at this time to ministering to the sick and pointing the people to God. The temples rolled in wealth from the offerings of the people who hoped to appease the wrath of the Cholera Goddess, many small temples being at this time built up into imposing structures. Dr. Green's tracts on cholera were distributed by thousands by the Government and his methods widely followed.

VI

1866–1879

"Laborers are few."

Apart from the vigorous work of the Medical Mission the history of the 60's is a rather depressing story. The Mission force was depleted. Mr. and Mrs. Quick and Mr. and Mrs. Hitchcock who reached the field in 1858 and Mr. and Mrs. Bates who came in '61 were all invalided home before their work was more than well begun. It was with poignant sorrow that they left the Mission already grown so dear to them, so promising and so needy. Several of the missionaries had been many years on the field and were working far beyond their strength. Late in the 60's Mr. and Mrs. DeRiemer joined the Mission and for nearly ten years worked hard and earnestly, usually at remote and lonely stations. Returning on furlough they did not rejoin the Mission. These were war times in America and funds were scarce.

The earnest effort to press the work in spite of all obstacles led to the introduction of new methods some of which proved of lasting value. The American and the British and Foreign Bible Societies had always given generous grants in payment of the expenses of distributing the Scriptures beginning as far back as 1821. Colporteurs had been employed extensively but in 1864 there is first mentioned the employment of Mary Thevany as "Bible Reader." Two years later the Uduvil school girls paid the salary of a "Bible Woman" who gave a part of her time, going among the women to read the Scriptures, sing, pray and invite them to worship the true God. In 1868 the second such worker was engaged at Uduvil and a year later the plan appears thoroughly established with Bible women elsewhere in the Mission.

In the 60's also, Youth's Associations, forerunners of the Christian Endeavor Societies of later days, were formed at all the stations, to include all the baptised children of the church. They exerted a strong influence for good through several years and many children were led to Christ. At two or three of the stations Christian congregations in addition to the church membership were formed as had been done long before in Tellippalai. At Vaddukoddai, under the leadership of the native pastor, the members of this congregation were divided among several church members for prayer, visitation and personal work, quite a number being brought into the church within a few months by this means. In 1862 a printed pastoral letter was prepared and the various Christian workers made a special effort to visit every family in their field and talk and pray with them, leaving one of the letters to be read and reread in the home. A special preaching effort was made again in 1868. The whole field was divided into two parts and each was put under the care of one of the missionaries for the evangelistic work. All the helpers in the field who were not

BIBLE WOMEN AT WORK

regularly stationed as preachers or pastors were assigned to the special effort. They went together to every village in turn and held a series of evening meetings, in the daytime visiting every house and making a loving presentation of the Gospel and inviting all the people to the public meeting at night.

At several of the stations the missionary women took charge of a Helping Hand Society, inviting the very poorest women dependent for their food on each day's labor to spend an afternoon each week on the Mission house veranda with the understanding that the time lost from their work would be paid for at the close of the year. Some conducted a sewing class with a Bible lesson and singing, others had the Gospel meeting only. This has been blest of God to the help and cheer of these women and to the salvation of some among them.

So marked had been the blessing attendant upon the Girls' school at Uduvil that it was determined to open a similar school for the girls in the outlying districts across "salt river." For four years about 1840 Mr. and Mrs. Apthorpe had carried on a little school at Varany with great success but that location had been judged too malarial for a permanent institution. Now in 1868 a new school was opened at Udupiddi and Miss Harriet Townshend came from America to superintend it. At the same time it was decided to take as many girls at Uduvil as could be accomodated without adding to the equipment and so to extend the benefits of a Christian training to much larger numbers.

Various expedients were tried for increasing the efficiency of the vernacular schools, now greatly reduced in numbers and supported wholly by American funds since Government Grants had been declined. An excellent plan followed for some years was that of grading the village school teachers by examinations and then outlining studies in which they were further examined at their regular teachers' meeting. In 1865 about twenty-five of them were invited to Vaddukoddai for a few weeks of special study in the Training School, a most profitable experiment. In 1860 there were 100 schools less than there were twenty-five years before. In 1859 the subject of grants was up for discussion and a council of native assistants was called to consider the matter.

By 1869 they were ready to try a new plan of supervision, the whole school system being turned over to one missionary in the hope of better efficiency, two missionaries at the same time being assigned to evangelistic work and one to the medical department. A year later a Board of Education was formed consisting of twelve members, pastors and laymen, who took full charge, then for the first time since 1855 receiving the grants which the Government had all along been willing to pay. Mr. Thos. Smith was made the manager of all the schools under this plan and to this Board were paid all the grants for all the schools, as well as the mission funds devoted to that work, to be distributed by it to the several schools in accordance with attendance, passes and other conditions agreed upon. This relieved the other missionaries of much labor but it also curtailed their authority in their own districts. New schools were opened, largely increasing the numbers and probably decreasing their Christian influence through the retention in some cases of the Hindu schoolmasters

THE HELPING HAND AT UDUVIL, 1908

with the schools taken over from them. For definite spiritual results effort was spread too thin. The one manager had 150 schools with 8000 children under his charge.

Miss Hester Hillis was the first to develop separate religious work under the charge of women. From 1870 to 1880 she was occupied with evangelistic work from house to house, chiefly in the Panditerippu field where there was no resident missionary family. Finding that she could provide food for several girls for the cost of the wages of the two servants she was employing, Miss Hillis took ten girls into her family with whom she shared food and shelter. She felt a peculiar interest in the low-caste people and longed to see them fully accepted into the family of Christ. The most valuable service she rendered was the training and inspiring of the young people whom she employed as helpers, some of whom still bear the marks of her Christian character and have been used of God to do for Him a thousand times what she ever did directly.

No record printed or written tells fairly what was accomplished by the faithful efforts of the missionary wives, many of them busy with the care of little children and all of them ministering to the comfort of the whole Mission in cordial hospitality. Their work took up the special nurture of the Christian women and in meetings with them and with the servants employed about the Mission houses and with the children of the station schools they spent many busy hours. They supervised and encouraged the Bible women at their stations, most of whom had no special training other than what they were able to give. Of one, Mrs. J. C. Smith, it was said: "Always in frail health and apparently of little use outside her quiet, orderly, cheerful home, her influence was seen spreading in gentle ripples wider and wider still." Her last words were: "Oh, I want all the people of Udupiddi to come to Christ, I do! I do!!" Similar testimony might be given of many whose names do not appear at all in the Mission records except with the date of the beginning and end of their service, but whose lives were fragrant with loving Christian ministeries.

Special mention should be made of the remarkable service rendered by Father and Mother Spaulding who lived and labored in Ceylon from 1819 to 1873 with but one visit to America of three years, a service paralleled in few lands and in few Missions. Mr. Spaulding contributed more in the way of literary work than any other member of the Mission in his day and his zeal and love were remarkable to the end. His influence over the forming character of the girls at Uduvil was marked and he had many sons and daughters in Christ.

After their death Miss Agnew continued the work at Uduvil to a most fruitful old age. In 1874 was held a notable Jubilee meeting where gathered hundreds of graduates and their families, an occasion of rejoicing to the whole Tamil people. It was found that 532 girls had been admitted to the school of whom 383 had become church members, practically every one who had compleated the full course. Of the whole number 365 were known to have married and a list was made indicating the positions occupied by their husbands, a remarkable showing as to the lasting influence of this school upon the ideals of a whole people. No influence has been more powerful for Christ than this, none so effective in breaking down the hindering superstitions of the people. The women of any land are its most conservative force and wise is the statesmanship that goes directly to them with the Gospel. Miss Agnew wrote of this occasion: "The crowning event of the Jubilee year was the reception of twenty-four of our precious charges to the commun- ion of the church. Pray for these little ones and for those who watch over them. It is a delightful work to train them." At Udupiddi too they were finding this a de- lightful work. Miss Townshend wrote of the new school as "a little garden in the wilderness, set with plants of hope."

JAFFNA COLLEGE

As time went on it became in- creasingly apparent that some provision must be made for higher English education. The Tamil men most interested, after long deliberation, presented a plan for a College which they hoped might meet the approval of the Mission as well as the public. From na- tive sources in Ceylon an endow- ment was to be raised amounting to £5000 and as much more from America. The buildings at Vad- dukoddai were to be turned over to the new "Jaffna College" and a Principal appointed by the American Board, the American missionaries being trustees of the institution. Every effort was to be made to safeguard the Christ- ian character of the new College.

This spontaneous effort on the

part of Tamil Christians was very gratifying and the very men who had opposed English education under the auspices of the Mission gladly co-operated with this movement. Substantially the above plan was adopted, modified so as to provide for a Board of Trustees incorporated in America to administer the funds collected there and a Board of Directors in Jaffna representing all three protestant Missions. A strong committee was formed to undertake the raising of the funds in Ceylon and Messrs. Sanders and Hastings at home on furlough made a good beginning in America, securing a strong Board and considerable amounts of money. Mr. Sanders returned to become Principal but died in 1871 before an actual beginning had been made and Rev. E. P. Hastings became, July 3, 1872, the first Principal of Jaffna College, the first missionary college founded in the field of the American Board. An associated but independent interest was that of the Vaddukoddai High School long successfully carried on under native Christian management. This was begun in 1857 and two years later four other schools were reported as having some four hundred pupils. When its Tamil principal, Mr. Robert Breckinridge became a Government Inspector of schools it was proposed to call a man from America to act in that capacity, his salary and expenses to be met locally from tuition and Government grants. This was done and Mr. Isaac Low came out to be Principal of the High School for four years. He was followed by Mr. H. Chapin but funds were insufficient to continue this plan.

The Training and Theological Institution begun at Vaddukoddai in 1858 was removed to Tellippalai in 1871 and placed under the care of Mr. Howland. Its chief value was in supplying teachers for the vernacular schools. It exerted a strong Christian influence and many of its students from heathen homes became Christians in spite of home opposition and greatly strengthened the Christian character of the village schools. As a Theological school it was not utilized except for one good class taken in 1875. This consisted of Mission helpers who kept on with their work, not residing in the school and were not regularly graduated. They were strong men however and though educated in Tamil only they have been among the most useful of the pastors. Still the limitations of such training were more and more felt and those who wanted to enter the ministry sought instruction at the Jaffna College where both languages were used.

The Mission now began to reap what it had sown, in the return for active service of its own loved sons and daughters. Mr. and Mrs. T. S. Smith joined in the work in 1870, Mr. and Mrs. S. W. Howland and Miss Susan Howland in 1873, Mr. Richard Hastings in 1879, and a few years later Miss Kate Hastings and Mr. Frank Sanders. No greeting as of strangers awaited these recruits but a warm welcome home. These missionary sons and daughters found they had a great advantage in the matter of language aquisition; not actually remembering it they were able to acquire it with greater effectiveness than others if not with greater ease. It is still remembered than Dr. Howland's first Tamil sermon like Dr. Poor's, was preached on the first anniversary of his arrival in Jaffna and Miss Howland's and Mr. Hasting's facility in the language has long been the wonder of those less fortunate. Dr. and Mrs. Howland brought a tent with them and entered heartily into practical evangelistic work in the villages. Their fresh and vigorous labors did much to cheer the time-worn veterans. Considerable re-adjustment of stations and work was necessary and somewhat frequent changes were made for a few years. The new missionaries however were not looking for hardships in their lot and Dr. Howland confided to the Secretary in Boston that the missionaries' home was "the happiest spot on earth."

VII

1880–1898

"God giveth increase."

With the coming of a fresh group of missionaries in 1880 new plans were projected into the work in Jaffna. Direct evangelism was then sweeping over North America under the inspiration of D. L. Moody's marvelous life. The Misses Leitch, accompanied by their brother, entered with earnestness and enthusiasm into this phase of the work which was already being pressed by the younger Howlands in Ceylon. Tent and village meetings, regular school visitation, study of the Bible widely stimulated by prizes and gifts, the development of the native singing with the help of Indian workers, all resulted in a quickened interest among the people and gave the opportunity to press home the Gospel message upon their hearts, so that large numbers were added to the church.

A strong temperance movement was a feature of the work at this time and in it the Misses Leitch gave valiant aid. Temperance lyrics and hymns were prepared and widely sung among children and adults. Mrs. John B. Gough contributed $800 for the prosecution of this special work. In 1888 Mrs. Mary C. Leavitt, W. C. T. U. round-the-world missionary visited the Jaffna field and greatly increased the interest in this subject. A foundation was laid for the stalwart opposition to the use of alcohol which a later generation has made so prominent.

During their seven years in Ceylon the Misses Leitch became convinced that one great need of the Mission was that of better equipment for its institutions, and they started in 1887 to collect funds in India, Scotland and England for the enlargement of the Jaffna College and for the establishment of a Medical Department to be connected with it as had been planned by Dr. Green many years before. This was authorized by the Mission but the plans soon outgrew the expectations of the Jaffna missionaries who were embarrassed by the receipt of larger funds than they saw how to expend wisely at that stage of the work. An extensive scholarship system was established at this time, and permanently endowed.

Ever since it was decided that Dr. Green could not return the Mission had been asking for another American physician to develop the Medical work. Their plan was to provide his salary locally, with the help of grants from the Government. Now, with the project for a Medical Department in the College well under way, Dr. and Mrs. Marston were sent from England to take charge of it. They lived in Jaffna town for a few months but not finding the unsettled conditions of the work satisfactory they gave it up and returned to England. Later the Medical Department was again separated from the College and established at Manepay, and Drs. T. B. Scott and Mrs. Mary E. M. Scott were secured to take charge. The funds collected by the Misses Leitch were turned over to the Board and the medical work was then made an integral part of the Mission and subject to its direction.

Uduvil school shared in the material benefits of this period, a large scholarship fund being collected by Mrs. S. W. Howland and another by the Misses Leitch. This was made necessary by the increase in fees which the school needed for its support even in addition to the large Government grants, and which many of the people were too poor to pay. A beautiful building designed to accommodate one hundred girls was erected, the gift of the Woman's Board of Missions with some misgivings as to whether the plans were not on too large a scale. The passing of only a few years rendered this large building wholly inadequate to the increasing demand for the education of girls under Christian influences. Here the training of women teachers was begun in 1885, a department of the work destined to exert a wide influence upon social and educational standards.

Tellippalai Training School was next rebuilt and partly equipped for industrial work, the main school building being named Sanders Hall in honor of Rev. M. D. Sanders who opened the school at Vaddukoddai in 1858. Uduvil church was also remodeled and rebuilt and in it were placed memorial tablets to many of the great missionary leaders who had passed away. All these extensive building operations were under the supervision of Rev. T. S. Smith. He gave to them years of hard and

JAFFNA COLLEGE ATHLETICS

CEYLON MISSIONARIES, 1890

often thankless service while carrying heavy burdens of church and school work as well. The old, old, Varany church was repaired and dedicated in 1894. Mr. Smith had been born there fifty years before and took great interest in presiding at the opening of the church.

Mr. Smith's great desire was to see an Industrial school built up at Tellippalai and to that end he secured (*for the use of the Training school boys*) equipment for carpentry, masonry and printing. He never achieved a real industrial school in the sense that the boys learned trades for their support in life but they received a useful manual training which helped, through Government grants, in their maintenance while in school. This department Mr. Smith developed on his own responsibility but after it was decided that his health would not permit him to return the Mission took over the whole enterprise so that the new missionary to be put in charge might not be embarrassed by work requiring separate support.

UDUVIL MEMORIAL CHURCH

Udupiddi school, remote and sheltered, was truly "a vine of the Lord's planting" and bore precious fruit of lives transformed. Its first Principal, Miss Harriet Townshend, in 1882, knowing that she must very soon die, called the girls one by one to her bedside to plead with them to accept Jesus Christ and had the joy of leading fourteen of them to the Saviour. No wonder she died in triumph and is still remembered with affection. Her work was taken up with real efficiency by Mrs. Richard Hastings who went to Udupiddi as a bride in 1883 and spent many happy years there training the Tamil girls of this district as well as the four daughters who came to her own home.

Miss Agnew, too, in 1883, laid her armor down, having fought a good fight and kept the faith to the end. Forty three years she lived among the Tamil people, dearer to her than her own and devoted her life to training their daughters for God. A strong, wise, consecrated woman, they called her "the mother of a thousand daughters" and the touch of her uncompromising yet loving spirit is still felt upon hundreds of homes and lives. Hers was a great life.

From 1880 to 1890 there was encouraging development of the native churches. The little congregations at Moolai, North Erlalai and South Erlalai were set off as separate churches, making fifteen in all, and no less than six Tamil pastors were ordained. These were Revs. W. P. Nathaniel, S. John,

TELLIPPALAI TRAINING SCHOOL 1901

UDUPIDDI BOARDING SCHOOL 1901

Wm. Joseph, S. Eliatamby, Isaac Paul, and S. Veerahatty. They had received their training in successive theological classes, one conducted in Tamil by Father Howland at Tellippalai, and a second instructed chiefly in English by Dr. Howland and Rev. T. P. Hunt at Chavakachcheri and finishing its work with Revs. E. P. Hastings and B. H. Rice at Vaddukoddai.

Self-support was continually urged upon the churches by the Board, and the Mission was often hard pressed between the demands from the Prudential Committee to cut down expenses—demands reasonable in America but not so reasonable in Ceylon — and demands from the field to increase them because of bank failures and other unforeseen conditions which cut off local resources. The first effort towards local support of the churches was made in 1856. By 1868 two of the churches were paying their pastors' full salary without help from the Mission, one other paid three-fourths and two more a half each. Ten years later eight had attained self-support and by 1882 only three of the fifteen pastors received any part of their salary from America. Thereafter progress was rapid; in 1900 only two of the eighteen churches received any help and considerable contributions were being made by the stronger churches for the help of those less strong.

The Board of Education which had charge of all the village schools was dissolved in 1883. Its work was good in some ways but time had shown that its power was too centralized and its action too slow. To develop local interest and responsibility separate committees were formed at each station to administer the school funds and control the schools, with the resident missionary as the nominal head responsible to the Government and to the Mission.

It was in 1893 that Dr. and Mrs. Scott came to Manepay to enter upon their work so needed and so blest of God. Heavy responsibilities of stations and schools were laid upon Dr. Scott in addition to the special medical work for which he came. Ample funds were available for repairing and rebuilding the hospital and this he undertook at once. He found his professional opportunities limited only by his strength and like Dr. Green he laid great emphasis upon the evangelistic side of the medical work. Mrs. Scott, herself a trained nurse as well as a doctor, began the training of Tamil Christian young women as nurses, in addition to a multitude of duties in connection with the hospital and her home.

At the same time the Misses Leitch returned to set on foot plans for a great hospital for women and children, for which they had collected funds and in which they had interested the Zenana Mission of England. This society works in connection with existing agencies in India, supplementing their general work with additional specialized effort among women, the whole remaining under the charge of the missions already at work. So in Jaffna it was proposed to build a hospital which should aid the work of all the Missions there. The American Mission gave the use of the vacant buildings at Chavakachcheri, the center of a very populous and neglected district. The house was repaired for the residence of the lady doctors but before the hospital was built, Dr. Leslie who had come from England for the work went to the large Government hospital for women in Colombo.

It was decided to establish the Zenana Mission Hospital in a more central and a more healthful location and a site was purchased at Inuvil, on the main traffic road of the Province and only a mile from Uduvil. Here beautiful and spacious buildings were erected and the whole plant finally turned over, a magnificent gift, to the American Board, the Zenana Mission relinquishing all claims. Dr. Isabella Curr from Scotland and Dr. Mary Irwin Rutnam from

MRS. M. E. M. SCOTT, M. D., AND NURSES

Canada were sent out to take up this special medical work for women. Dr. Rutnam soon left to join her husband in Colombo and to enter upon the private practice of her profession there. In Sept., 1898, the McLeod Hospital for women and children was formally opened at Inuvil with Dr. Curr in charge.

A serious situation now developed because of the lessened number of ordained missionaries. Father Howland passed away in 1892 after forty-six years of devoted service. His later years when strength was feeble were perhaps the most fruitful of all in their influence upon the minds of a people instinctively reverent to old age. For a year Rev. Ernest Bell worked with enthusiasm but he left the field before he ever mastered the language. In 1898, Dr. and Mrs. Howland, well loved and better known among the people than most other missionaries because of their residence at every station in the course of twenty-seven years' service, were obliged to return to America on account of Mrs. Howland's health. Mr. and Mrs. Smith went on furlough in 1898, leaving only Mr. Hastings and Dr. Scott to do the work of at least five men. It was again seriously discussed in America whether the Mission should not be given up, a possibility which took the heart out of the workers, but in 1898 the Prudential Committee finally decided to strengthen the force and to invest money enough to continue the work with reasonable hope of success. Mr. and Mrs. Holton were sent over by the Madura Mission to fill the gap and the heavy burdens were readjusted to be carried till the coming of a strong re-enforcement in 1899.

THE MCLEOD HOSPITAL, INUVIL, 1897

When the Mission is shorthanded it is always the evangelistic work that suffers, not because it is considered less important but because the institutional work of schools, college, hospitals, cries out for attention with an appeal that cannot even temporarily be evaded. The one compensating fact is that this draws out the efforts of the Tamil Christians and so it was at this period of reduced numbers in the Missionary force. From six men and eight women missionaries in 1885 the numbers gradually declined to two men and five women in 1898—during about the same period ten Tamil pastors were ordained. Besides these previously mentioned they were Revs. F. Arketell, C. M. Sanders, J. M. Sanders, D. Valupillai, S. Abraham, R. Bryant. Great interest throughout the whole province was aroused by the return from India of a brilliant young lawyer, C. Chellayahpillai. He was a native of Jaffna, but had spent most of his life in India, a reckless, ungodly life, until he came under the preaching of the saintly Bowen, and soon after was converted in a meeting of the Salvation Army in Madras. He entered into a clear experience of Bible Holiness, and after first winning his wife to Christ, came on a visit to Jaffna, and went like a flame of fire among his countrymen and relatives, calling them to repentance and bringing many to God.

The Ceylon Mission has always been a pioneer in new movements. The fact has already been mentioned that in this field were founded the first Boarding Schools for girls on foreign missionary soil and the first College connected with the American Board, as well as the earliest indigenous Home Missionary organization, called here the Native Evangelical Society. This was formed by the missionaries in 1832 and turned over to be officered and managed

WORK OF THE NATIVE EVANGELICAL SOCIETY

THE FIRST Y. M. C. A IN ASIA

wholly by the Tamil Christians and to provide for the religious work in the islands off-lying from Jaffna. In 1899, following a visit of George Sherwood Eddy, a Students' Mission was organized to operate in a field selected on the mainland. This was also a pioneer, the forerunner of the India National Missionary Society which was soon to press the claims of India's unevangelized millions upon India's Christian sons. The same year a Women's Foreign Missionary Society began to gather funds and to co-operate in prayer and plans with the Students' Mission.

It should also be recorded here that in 1884, Prof. Frank Sanders began at Jaffna College the first regularly organized Y. M. C. A. in Asia and that a year later at Uduvil the Misses Leitch organized the first Christian Endeavor Society in missionary lands.

VIII
1899–1915

"Workers together with Him."

Roused at last to the necessity for immediate relief in the Ceylon Mission the Prudential Committee in 1899 authorized the sending of six recruits, Rev. G. G. and Mrs. Clara Brown, Dr. Annie Young, Miss Helen I. Root and Rev. J. H. and Mrs. Frances Dickson. The Jaffna College which had been under the temporary charge of Mr. W. E. Hitchcock was put in the care of Rev. R. C. Hastings, the beloved son of its first Principal. Mr. and Mrs. Brown were sent to Udupiddi to care for the Girls' school and the station work, Dr

MRS. BROWN AT UDUPIDDI

Young to strengthen the medical work at Inuvil and to open a dispensary at Chavakachcheri, Miss Root to aid Miss Howland at Uduvil and Mr. and Mrs. Dickson to take charge of the whole missionary enterprise at Tellippalai.

In 1901 a second Deputation was sent from the American Board, consisting of the Foreign Secretary, Dr. James L. Barton, Mrs. Barton, Rev. J. F. Loba, a Congregational pastor, and Mr. W. F. Whittemore, a business man from Boston. They spent a month with the Ceylon Mission, visiting all the stations and preaching in nearly every church, gaining acquaintance with all the pastors, meeting hundreds of the Tamil Christians and many Hindus, and carefully studying the whole situation. Their fellowship in Christ and the frank consideration of all the difficulties by which the Mission was confronted greatly cheered the missionaries and resulted in a clearer understanding on the part of the Prudential Committee of the needs and the possibilities of the work in Ceylon.

It was recognized that the Mission could not do justice to the printing work which conditions forced upon it without larger and better equipment. After careful consideration of all the interests involved it was therefore decided to give the Tamil firm then in possession of the old Mission Press at Manepay one year more of grace to put the plant in order to do really good work. Failing this the Mission bought back the press and type and business which it had sold so many years before. Tons of type now useless were destroyed and much of the equipment was found to be hopelessly out of date. It was also determined to develop the Tellippalai School not as an Industrial school but as a Normal school and to maintain the Press as an associated industry whereby students could partly support themselves during their course and acquire a knowledge of the printing business which might later be of great value to them. For their manual work in connection with the Press considerable grants-in-aid were continued as the school still conformed to Government requirements for an Industrial school while pursuing its own course as a Normal Training school. Through the persistent energy of Mr. Dickson and with generous aid from friends in America the whole plant was thoroughly overhauled and rebuilt, new presses installed, large printing contracts undertaken, millions of pages of Christian literature turned out and employment furnished to numbers of worthy students. The profit from its commercial contracts maintains the Press as a Christian agency and its influence through the wide dissemination of Christian truth has given the Mission again a commanding position in this regard.

During the last quarter of the century there has been a succession of visits from preachers and evangelists from America and India and England which have done much to deepen the spiritual life of the church. The list includes such Christian leaders as Mr. Grubb of England, Messrs. Wishard, Mott, Wilder, W. W. White and Sherwood Eddy of America and many fellow missionaries from the India field. Foreign officers of the Salvation Army have also conducted meetings of spiritual profit. In 1900 the first formal conference of Christian women workers was held at Uduvil where the Bible women, now more than sixty in number, gathered for three days with the missionaries and other leaders. Miss Eva Swift, head of the Lucy Perry Noble Bible School in Madura, came to conduct a series of Bible studies and the whole work was greatly stimulated thereby. Other conferences of power and far-reaching influence have since been held, some for women and some for men, often with no outside speakers but always with the presence and help of the Lord and greatly to the betterment of spiritual conditions.

Long years the churches had gone on without an accounting with their membership lists. In 1901 began a serious attempt to purify the rolls, and many names were dropped, many memberships transferred, and a considerable reduction in numbers reported. This wholesome pruning resulted almost at once in new vigor of growth.

One of the recommendations made by the Deputation and one in accord with the deepest desire of the missionaries was that a campaign of aggressive evangelism be undertaken with a special view to pressing home the truth of the Gospel upon the hearts of those already well instructed in the Bible. It was apparent, however, that with so small a force of foreign workers their time must necessarily be spent largely in the work of the great institutions for which they alone could be responsible. The field needed a specialized evangelistic worker, either Tamil or American, Spirit-filled, soul-burdened, who should lead in this movement. The pastor of the Uduvil church, long associated with the Gospel ministry was set apart for one year with good results in this field but it was too great a strain upon his health and could not be continued. The pressing problem of evangelistic leadership has not yet been solved. Strong and efficient workers among the Tamil Christians are coming to the fore and the need is much upon the hearts of those who live near to God.

A very insistent temperance sentiment has been aroused during the past few years among all classes of the people. This is in opposition to the plans of the Government in relation to the Excise question and has brought its promoters somewhat into disfavor. The Christian community is making remarkable progress toward total abstinence as a standard of Christian living. Hindus as well have demonstrated their willingness to dispense with the profits of the palmyra toddy for the sake of the welfare of their neighbors.

The old Uduvil School met successfully in 1902 a crisis in its history when by the unanimous vote of the Mission a "low-caste" girl was received as a regular boarding pupil. In the face of severe opposition on the part of some Christians and of practically all the Hindu community, through persistent kindness and loyalty to the spirit of Christ and with the co-operation of many earnest Christians among the people, the matter was carried through and the point established that no caste observance could be tolerated in this Christian institution. A similar undertaking at the Boys' Training School at Tellippalai came to a like successful issue. For two years, on account of the illness of supervising missionaries the Udupiddi Girls' Boarding School was moved to Uduvil and all the girls taught as one school. While this gave unusual advantages to the girls who came it was found that new girls whom it was especially desired to reach with the training of a Christian home were not being brought to the more distant school and as soon as possible the school was reopened at Udupiddi where under the care successively of Mrs. Hitchcock and Mrs. Ward it still does as it always has done a peculiarly gracious work for the young women for that part of the field.

The return of Miss Julia Green in 1906 to the former home of her parents was an occasion of rejoicing to the people and to the Mission, and a few years later a royal welcome was given Miss Minnie Hastings not only a daughter but a granddaughter of the Mission. With Miss Lula Bookwalter she shared

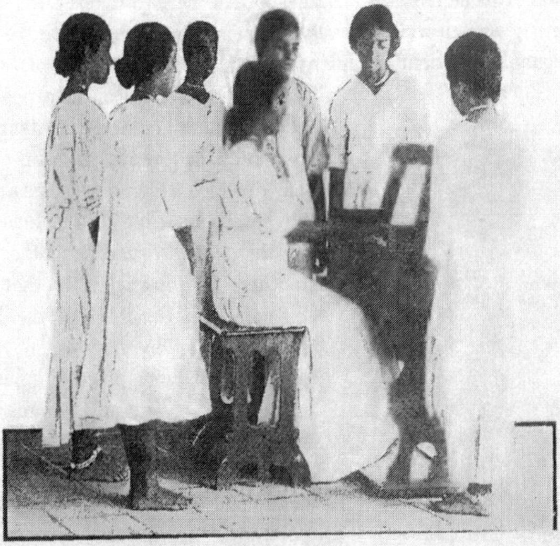

UDUVIL SCHOOL GIRLS

in the later expansion of Uduvil both in course of study and in material equipment. In 1913 Miss Susan Howland after thirty-five years as Principal of the Uduvil School asked to be released from her duties there to take up the evangelistic work among women which many years before she had come to the field to do. She began her patient, loving visitation of the hundreds of homes where the wife and mother, possibly the grandmother and the daughter had been her pupils and in every one of which a loving welcome awaited her. Inheritor of the love felt by the people toward her father and mother and toward her brother and his wife, this daughter of the Mission has won by her own devoted and faithful life a place of influence not granted to any other among the missionary force. In 1909 in connection with the celebration of the centennial of Miss Agnew's birth a portrait of her loved successor was unveiled in the Uduvil School thus linking the lives of two who have been permitted to serve God there through seventy-five years.

MISS JULIA E. GREEN

In 1902 the few feeble Christian Endeavor Societies outside the Uduvil School were united and greatly stimulated in their work. The India Secretaries were invited to visit Ceylon, Rev. F. Hatch from America and Rev. H. Halliwell from England, new societies were formed, old ones were divided and made more efficient, representatives were sent to the great conventions in India, union in this particular of the work was brought about between the Church Mission young people and those of the American Mission, and the whole enterprise put under the charge of a Tamil Christian Endeavor Secretary. Membership in these societies in Ceylon has usually been confined to the girls in the Boarding Schools, the young women at home who have been members while in school and the little boys and girls in the several churches. An unusual and striking feature of the Christian Endeavor work in Ceylon has been the series of general Rallies occurring several times a year and bringing together scores of enthusiastic young women who have very few other opportunities for real fellowship with others of their own age.

MISS SUSAN R. HOWLAND

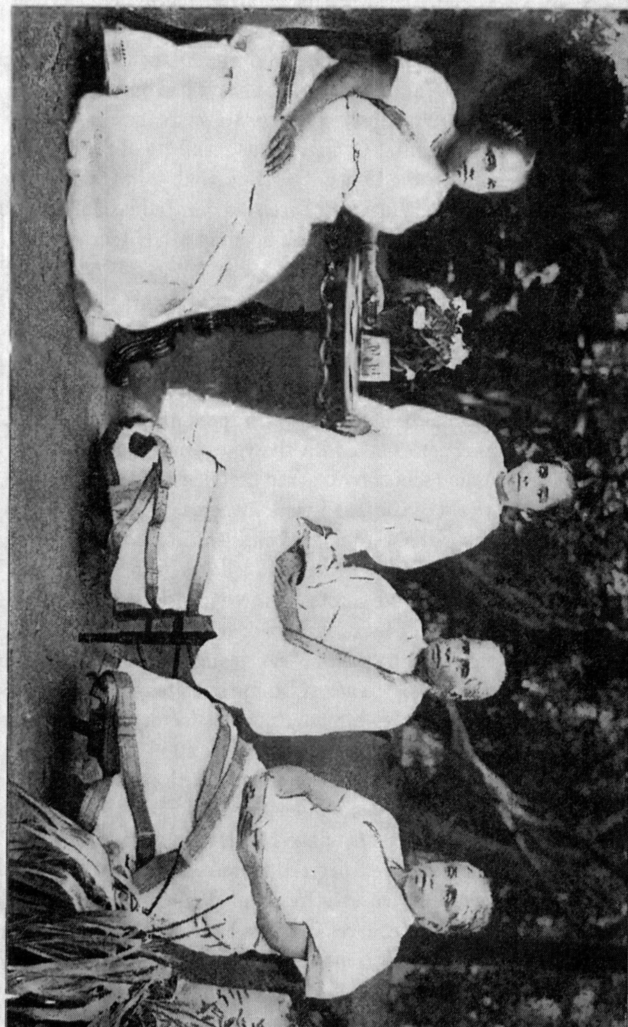

FOUR GENERATIONS TAUGHT AT UDUVIL

The Young Men's Christian Association makes its appeal to the older boys and young men in the College and in the villages. Good Associations are maintained at several points, of much influence upon the lives of young men. Co-operation with other Missions has been well developed along the line of the Y. M. C. A. and student camps and conferences have been of great value.

It was Prof. Frank Sanders, himself a son of the Mission, under whom the Y. M. C. A. work opened. Jaffna College has always had one or two American professors in addition to its Principal. During late years they have been regularly appointed by the Prudential Committee as members of the Mission and assigned to special service in the College. Before that they were under appointment from the American Board of Directors for Jaffna College. Their names follow and except for the longer appointment of Mr. Hitchcock they have served from two years to four years each: Messrs. W. E. Hitchcock, F. K. Sanders, Irving R. Wood, J. A. Sliver, Wm. Marsh, W. W. Wallace, I. L. Best, T. A. Elmer, John Bicknell, A. A. Ward, L. B. Fritts, Harry York, and Charles Miller. These young men have taken great interest in the religious life and the life in general of the college boys and have been an inspiration to the work of the Y. M. C. A. To them also these short term appointments in close association with the older missionaries and with the young manhood of Jaffna have proved an excellent training school for marked usefulness in this and other mission fields and in the world of Christian work at home.

Through many years plans were under consideration looking to the union of Jaffna College with all the other Protestant colleges in the Province. Various difficulties have prevented the success of these plans and it has been determined to develop the higher educational work of the Mission through Jaffna College itself. For many years this College maintained its own standards and granted its own diplomas. Then it bcame affiliated with Calcutta University and degrees were given to a number of satisfactory students, some of whom achieved real distinction. Later this connection with Calcutta was broken by a ruling of the Educational Commission with reference to the areas from which students of the various universities might be drawn. It proved impossible to meet the requirements of the Madras University for full affilliation though some students gained degrees there. The examinations of the London and Cambridge Universities were ill-adapted to the needs of Tamil students. Of late years all the colleges in Jaffna have been obliged temporarily to occupy themselves with work somewhat under college grade, pending the establishment by the Government of a Ceylon University with which they may affiliate.

One serious gap in the educational system of the Mission has been stopped by the decision to unite the Vaddukoddai English high school with the College and to take boys of all ages as regular pupils, thus making it possible for Christian parents to keep their boys in the one institution from the beginning to the end of their schooling. This adds many responsibilities in the mis-

DR. ISABELLA CURR AND NURSES

sionary supervision of the College but increases largely the possiblilty of effective training in Christian character.

Dr. Harry York, foreign professor in the College from 1908 to 1913, offered the plan of correlating the eight English schools of the Mission as preparatory to the College with a uniform standard of work and supervision. Mr. Chas. Miller, a Normal graduate, was sent in 1914 to carry this plan to success. Dr. York also developed a series of practical Teachers' Institutes for all the English schools of the Mission with prepared papers, discussions and practice teaching calculated to help in raising professional ideals.

In 1903 occurred an event of far-reaching significance when under the kindly persistence of Mr. Brown the Ecclesiastical Body of long standing was re-organized into a permanent Council, a delegated body composed of Tamil ministers, laymen and missionaries, which should meet regularly to hear reports from the churches, maintain discipline, develop new work, and raise and disburse funds for the aid of weak churches. Funds voted by the Mission from money supplied by the Board were put in the hands of the Council for distribution. The functions of the Council have developed as new needs have arisen. Changes in the pastorate are now made through its agency and on the whole there has been cordial co-operation with its plans. After several years an invitation was accepted to join the South India United Church, comprising the churches there of the Free Church of Scotland, the Dutch Reformed Church of America, the London Missionary Society of England, the Church of Scotland and the American Board in Madura and Ceylon. These Tamil speaking Christians, generally alike in doctrine and practice, have united in a real fellowship each remaining under the direction of its own Board. This union with large numbers of believers has done much to broaden the Christian love of the Jaffna church, too long isolated from others of like faith. Increasing practical and spiritual efficiency on the part of the South India United Church is confidently to be expected. Already students have enjoyed the training offered by the United Theological Seminary at Bangalore and are at work in the home field with a broader outlook than could have been gained with the best of training there.

The pastors ordained during the past few years are Revs. S. R. Hitchcock, J. K. Chinnatamby and E. T. Williams. Under direction of the Council extensive evangelistic efforts have been put forth and the out-lying churches strengthened.

The whole people of Jaffna recognize their debt to the Mission and among the churches there is a cordial willingness to assume financial responsibilities in connection with its work. Quite remarkable increase in giving for the support of pastors and for the aid of weak churches has been seen within the past ten years and the end is not yet.

In 1906 it was undertaken to raise a Centenary Fund looking to the celebration of 1916, a part to be collected each year and put at interest with the expectation that the sum might then amount to Rs. 20000, this to be used as a

GREEN HOSPITAL STAFF, 1905

permanent fund for strengthening Christian work in Ceylon. The gathering in of this money has each year since been a feature of much interest at the October meeting. In addition to this at the time of the A. B. C. F. M. Centennial the sum of Rs. 4000 was raised by the Tamil Christians themselves and sent to the Board, as a thank offering for all the good which God had done through its agency in Ceylon. A similar thankoffering of Rs. 1000 was presented at the Centenary of the British and Foreign Bible Society.

CLASS AT UDUVIL

IX
1916

"White already to harvest."

Through a full century the Gospel has been taught and preached and lived by our missionaries in Ceylon. It remains to consider the conditions of today and the prospects for the future.

The land was long ago possessed in the name of Jesus Christ. The soil has been faithfully prepared, the seed sown. A partial harvest has been gathered and there is assurance that far larger things await the husbandmen.

There has been remarkable expension of the English school at Uduvil. This institution opened by Miss K. L. E. Myers in 1897 met a long felt want. From a little separate class taught upon the verandah it grew and grew until it out numbered the original vernacular Boarding School. Twice during the years when the Calcutta University gave its Local Examinations in Ceylon this school won the Chesab Chundra Sen Prize for the student having the highest standing of all the girl candidates in India, Burma and Ceylon.

Excellent results have since been attained in the Cambridge Local Examinations. A trained kindergartener, Miss Lucy Clarke has been added to the staff to carry on the work for little children begun under the supervision of Mrs. J. H. Dickson. To comply with the Government requirements as well as safely and conveniently to house the constantly augumenting numbers of students, the project was seriously undertaken in 1911 of providing a building suited to the new conditions. Meanwhile the building designed to accommodate one hundred girls took in twice that number and then another hundred and overflowed into a rented house near by. A good infirmary was built and temporary school rooms and still the need increased. An appeal was made to the people who had so richly enjoyed the benefits of the schools through generations and considerable funds were collected locally. The Women's Board came to the rescue and placed the needed new building among the needs to be met from the Golden Anniversary Gift. No school in all the world offers finer opportunities for building Christian character than has this school through all its history. Heir to all the noble traditions of the past the new Uduvil enters confidently upon the new century.

During recent years a vigorous opposition to the Christian schools has developed on the part of the Hindu community. Within a mile of Uduvil a fine building was erected for a Hindu boarding school for girls. Though appeal is made to the people on the ground of national and religious loyalty it has not secured the confidence even of Hindu parents to any extent detrimental to the Uduvil school. In some localities Hindu village schools were built so well equipped and so well supported that the Mission could hardly hope to compete

UDUVIL SCHOOL IN 1916

successfully with them. Meanwhile the Mission policy has been to select schools promising permanent usefulness and as fast as funds could be secured from America to put these one at a time into thoroughly good condition and there to hold the situation even if some other schools had to be temporarily or even entirely given up. Under this plan the schools of the whole field are gradually though too slowly assuming a position of greater influence.

VILLAGE VERNACULAR SCHOOL

These vernacular day schools have varied greatly as to numbers through the hundred years. Before the end of 1816, 80 pupils were enrolled and then for twenty years there was a steady and large increase until there were 6025 in 1836. Then came retrenchment and later a change in policy so that the numbers dropped to 1816 in 1856. From that time there has been constant advance, past the ten thousand mark, to 10462 in 1914. Yet this priceless opportunity for presenting Christ to the hearts of a friendly people has never been adequately improved. Supervision and equipment have never been sufficient to the task. Many faithful teachers have taught the Bible lessons when to do it threatened the lessening of their own salaries received from the Government grants. Many faithful missionaries and pastors have utilized the schools as meeting places and have presented the Gospel on Sundays and in the evenings to thousands upon thousands of hearers. The Word of God has been taught more generally perhaps than in any other mission field. It is the profound conviction of those who know the facts that the harvest is ripe and that the village schools offer a field most inviting to those who would gather sheaves for God.

It has been a long struggle at Tellippalai to furnish a satisfactory normal training because the boys of better ability all desired to have an English education. Some not able to afford the expense of that have come to Tellippalai and happily lack of means does not imply lack of brains and many good students have taken at least a part of their training there. English has of late years been taught in connection with the vernacular studies required for the Normal course. It is now proposed to have a union Training school under Government auspices at Copay. This will utilize the plant of the Church Mission Training School there and make possible an institution of much higher grade than the Missions could maintain separately. The younger boys will continue to be taught at Tellippalai where special emphasis will be placed upon Christian ideals and character.

With the opening of the new century and under the charge of a new Principal, Rev. John A. Bicknell, it is proposed to widen the scope of the Jaffna College. As always it represents the educational interests and the Christian ideals of the Tamil community. Donations have been secured locally sufficient to warrant the investment of large sums from America. New buildings are under construction, thorough equipment will be provided and the staff of teachers strengthened. Large plans are under way for its upbuilding and extension. Through the Y. M. C. A. the Vaddukoddai church and the resident missionaries, Christ is constantly set before the students and numbers of them yield their lives to Him.

Late years have completely demonstrated the practicability of the hospital methods adopted by Dr. and Mrs. Scott and Dr. Curr. In 1906 a branch hospital was opened in the populous island of Karadive lying to the west of the Jaffna peninsula. For some time it was kept as a memorial to Dr. S. F. Green and it did a good though never a large work under the administration of dispensers trained at Manepay and stationed there. As years passed the conviction grew upon the Medical department that the whole medical work was really a memorial to Dr. Green and with the concurrence of the Mission, Dr. Scott named the large hospital at Manepay the Green Memorial Hospital. The McLeod Hospital for women and children at Iduvil was also much enlarged and these two institutions have responded magnificently to the opportunities before them of ministering to those physically sick and spiritually lost. Among scores of valued Mission helpers it is surely not invidious to mention two, Dr. Albert K. M. Curtis at Manepay and Dr. Nallamma Murusasan at Inuvil who so multiplied the usefulness of the hospitals by their professional skill, their Christian devotion and their peculiar acceptability to their own country people.

DR. CURTIS

The training of Tamil nurses begun by Mrs. Scott in 1894 and carried on at both hospitals has sent scores of Christian young women on ministries of love among their own people and their dignity and efficiency in this new situation have made nursing and midwifery honorable where once they were considered unsuited to decent educated women.

NURSES AND THEIR CHARGES

The work of the medical department as a whole has increased from 135 hospital patients and 4247 dispensary treatments in 1896 to 3201 in-patients and 15012 treatments in 1914. A marked financial success has been achieved in both hospitals by making a reasonable charge for medicines and treatment, for operations and for room rent. None of these charges are burdensome and those too poor to pay them are treated free. Under this system all the running expenses of the hospital are met, including the salaries of the Tamil assistants. After the regretted return to America of Dr. and Mrs. Scott in 1913 it was impossible to continue the work at Manepay upon the same scale as before but that at Inuvil has grown and prospered. Dr. Curr's work is recognized throughout the Island and her patients are drawn from all communities and her nurses-in-training from all the missions. While every village in Jaffna is now open to the Christian missionary it is still the physician who has easiest access to the homes and hearts of the people.

The past few years have seen the rehabilitation of many of the church buildings in the Ceylon Mission. With financial prosperity came the desire to provide worthy houses of worship. The Navaly Christians without foreign aid carried through the building of a beautiful and suitable church and smaller ones were erected at Araly and Valanai. The latter was the gift of one devoted Christian man, a thankoffering to God for health restored. At Tellippalai the old historic church was rebuilt into a commodious and beautiful edifice. Others were extensively repaired.

The opening of railway communication with Colombo and with India brought new influences to bear upon the community and complicated the missionary problem. In closer touch with the life of the great Oriental ports and attracted by urban ideals, not all of them the best, the people of Jaffna lost something of simplicity and acquired much of worldliness. Ease of access however brought more freqvent visits from other missionaries and from officers of the Boards which proved of great value to the Christian people. They were intensely interested to see and hear the Home Secretary of the American Board, Dr. Patton, the Secretary, Miss Lamson and the Treasurer, Miss Day of the Woman's Board of Missions, the Editorial Secretary, Dr. Strong, and the honored President of the A. B. C. F. M., Dr. Capen, as they came to Jaffna on successive deputations.

More marked perhaps than in other fields has been the effect upon this whole people, comparatively isolated and remote, of the steady, patient presentation of Christian standards. Practices once common in Ceylon and still prevalent among the Tamils of South India are no longer tolerated here. Social standards have been greatly modified. Especially noticeable is the gradual raising of the age of marriage, not by law but by custom. The people have almost unconsciously yielded to Christian ideals even when they have not personally become Christians.

The church in Ceylon confronts not only the problems of all fields in non-Christian countries but those as well of all long established Christian communities. It must contend with heathenism all around it and with worldliness within itself. In Ceylon, India, America, everywhere the wheat and tares grow together.

No more pressing problem confronts the Mission than that of supplying spiritual leadership in the effort to stem the rising tide of worldliness in the church. Of especial value in this respect were the evangelistic meetings carried on by Mr. George Sherwood Eddy in 1915 in connection with the India campaign. Careful preparation preceded them and God's blessing was upon them. Following the Edinburgh Conference on Missions and at the invitation of its Continuation Committee members of the Ceylon Mission greatly profited by a careful study of the conditions of their field and by a deliberate consideration of its needs. All were convinced that God had set them in a harvest field already ripe, that other men had labored and they had entered into their labors. They realized that immediate and far-reaching results would follow if the claims of Christ could be faithfully pressed home upon the hearts of a people already thoroughly instructed in Bible truth and needing only the Holy Spirit's power to convince them of their need. This is the challenge of the new century.

For many, many years two great church gatherings have been held, the annual meeting of the Native Evangelical Society, that earliest of Home Missionary societies formed within the field of operations of the American Board, a meeting where the theme is personal responsibility for evangelism and where the program is in charge of Tamil men, and the other the "October meeting" held at the time of the meeting in America of the A. B. C. F. M. This is a great day when humanity's need for Christ and His salvation is brought home and where the Jaffna church recognizes and realizes its kinship with the church of God throughout the world. Hundreds of Christians attend these gatherings annually, renewing their fellowship with one another and reaffirming their allegiance to their Lord.

It was a little band of seven missionaries who undertook in 1816 the heroic task of proclaiming Christ to the Tamils of Ceylon. They have been followed in true apostolic succession by more than a hundred others all committed to the same great undertaking. Could all these unite with the multitude of Tamil Christians who in 1916 celebrate together the death and deathless love of Jesus, how they would rejoice that they were counted worthy to sow the seed which is the Word, to water it with their tears and to make possible the harvest divinely promised to those who faint not.

THE AMERICAN CEYLON MISSION IN 1916

Tamil Pastors and their Charges

*Rev. C. M. Cornelius	Karadive	1855–1861
*Rev. T. P. Hunt	Chavakachcheri	1855–1872
	Jaffna College	1872–1880
	Chavakachcheri	1880–1903
*Rev. D. Stickney	Valanai	1858–1864
	Udupiddi	1864–1901
	Alaveddi	1901–1905
*Rev. F. Asbury	Navaly	1860–1898
*Rev. B. H. Rice	Vaddukoddai	1867–1905
*Rev. A. Anketell	Tellippalai	1870–1877
*Rev. M. Welch	Alaveddi	1870–1885
*Rev. A. Bryant	Sanganai	1872–1898
*Rev. J. Christmas	Chavakachcheri	1873–1880
	Tellippalai	1880–1904
*Rev. H. Hoisington	Uduvil	1874–1891
	N. Erlalai	1895–1901
*Rev. S. John	Moolai	1880–1894
Rev. W. P. Nathaniel	Manepay	1881–1905
	Alaveddi	1905–1913
	Araly	1913–
Rev. S. Eliatamby	Panditerippu	1884–1891
	Uduvil	1891–
Rev. W. Joseph	N. Erlalai	1886–1897
	Jaffna College	1897–1905
	Vaddukoddai	1905–1910
	Navaly	1910–1915
	Manepay	1915–
Rev. Isaac Paul	S. Erlalai	1888–1901
	Valanai	1901–1906
	India	1906–1910
	Karadive	1910–
Rev. S. Veerakatty	Navaly	1888–1896
	Training School	1896–1902
	Tellippalai	1902–1910
	Vaddukoddai	1910–
*Rev. C. M. Sanders	Karadive	1891–1906
	Chavakachcheri	1906–1908
	Valanai	1908–1910
Rev. F. Anketell	Alaveddi	1891–1904
	Kangesanturai	1905–1910
	Manepay	1910–1915
	Udupiddi	1915–

*Rev. J. M. Sanders	Atchuvaly	1892–1906
	Udupiddi	1906–1912
Rev. D. Valupillai	Panditerippu	1894–1905
	Manepay	1905–1910
	Tellippalai	1910–
Rev. R. Bryant	Navaly	1896–1909
	Chavakachcheri	1909–1913
	Valanai	1913–
Rev. S. Abraham	Nunavil	1896–1899
	Straits Settlements	1899–
Rev. R. Hitchcock	Chavakachcheri	1906–1906
	Atchuvaly	1906–1910
	Valanai	1910–1913
	Udupiddi	1913–1915
	Navaly	1915–
Rev. J. K. Chinnatamby	Panditerippu	1909–1913
	Chavakachcheri	1913–
Rev. E. T. Williams	Atchuvaly	1915–

*Deceased.

Missionaries of the American Board

CEYLON MISSIONS

With the dates of their entering and leaving the service.

1. Rev. Edward Warren 1816–1818
2. Rev. James Richards 1816–1822
3. Mrs. Sarah Richards 1816–1825
4. Rev. Benjamin C. Meigs 1816–1857
5. Mrs. Sarah M. Meigs 1816–1840
6. Rev. Daniel Poor 1816–1855
7. Mrs. Susan B. Poor 1816–1821
8. Mrs. Ann K. Poor 1823–1855
9. Rev. Miron Winslow 1820–1836
10. Mrs. Harriet M. Winslow 1820–1833
11. Rev. Levi Spaulding 1820–1873
12. Mrs. Mary E. Spaulding 1820–1874
13. Rev. Henry Woodward 1820–1834
14. Miss Lydia M. Woodward 1820–1825
15. Mrs. Clarissa E. Woodward 1827–1836
16. Rev. John Scudder, M. D. 1820–1836
17. Mrs. Harriet Scudder 1820–1836
18. Rev. George A. Apthorpe 1833–1844
19. Mrs. Mary R. Apthorpe 1833–1849
20. Rev. Henry R. Hoisington 1833–1844
21. Mrs. Nancy L. Hoisington 1833–1844
22. Rev. Wm. Todd 1833–1834
23. Mrs. Lucy Todd 1833–1834
24. Rev. Samuel Hutchings 1833–1843
25. Mrs. Elizabeth Hutchings 1833–1843
26. Nathan Ward, M. D. 1833–1847
27. Mrs. Hannah Ward 1833–1847
28. Rev. James R. Eckard 1834–1843
29. Mrs. Margaret B. Eckard 1834–1843
30. Mr. Eastman S. Minor 1834–1850
31. Mrs. Lucy B. Minor 1834–1837
32. Mrs. Judith T. Minor 1839–1850
33. Rev. Alanson G. Hall 1835–1835
34. Mrs. Frances L. Hall 1835–1835
36. Rev. John Jay Lawrence 1835–1835
37. Mrs. Mary H. Lawrence 1835–1835
38. Rev. John M. S. Perry 1835–1837
39. Mrs. Harriet I. L. Perry 1835–1837
40. Miss Eliza Agnew 1840–1883
41. Miss Sarah F. Brown 1840–1841

42. Rev. Edward Cope 1840–1848
43. Mrs. Emily R. Cope 1840–1848
44. Rev. John C. Smith 1842–1872
45. Mrs. Eunice M. Smith 1842–1842
46. Mrs. Mary L. Smith 1844–1872
47. Rev. Robert Wyman 1842–1844
48. Mrs. Martha E. Wyman 1842–1844
49. Rev. Samuel G. Whittlesey 1842–1847
50. Mrs. Anna E. Whittlesey 1842–1848
51. Rev. Adin H. Fletcher 1846–1850
52. Mrs. Elizabeth W. Fletcher 1846–1850
53. Rev. Wm. W. Howland 1846–1892
54. Mrs. Susan R. Howland 1846–1887
55. Miss Mary A. Capell 1846–1848
56. Rev. Wm. W. Scudder 1847–1852
57. Mrs. Catharine H. Scudder 1847–1849
58. Rev. Eurotas P. Hastings 1847–1890
59. Mrs. Anna C. Hastings 1853–1891
60. Samuel F. Green, M. D. 1847–1874
61. Mrs. Margaret W. Green 1862–1874
62. Rev. Joseph T. Noyes 1849–1852
63. Mrs. Elizabeth A. Noyes 1849–1852
64. Rev. Cyrus T. Mills 1849–1853
65. Mrs. Susan T. Mills 1849–1853
66. Mr. Thos. S. Burnell 1849–1855
67. Mrs. Martha L. Burnell 1849–1855
68. Rev. Marshall D. Sanders 1852–1871
69. Mrs. Georgiana K. Sanders 1852–1868
70. Mrs. Caroline Sanders 1871–1871
71. Rev. Nathan L. Lord 1853–1858
72. Mrs. Laura W. Lord 1853–1858
73. Rev. Milan H. Hitchcock 1858–1861
74. Mrs. Lucy A. Hitchcock 1858–1861
75. Rev. James Quick 1858–1868
76. Mrs. Maria E. Quick 1858–1868
77. Rev. James A. Bates 1861–1863
78. Sarah A. L. Bates 1861–1863
79. Miss Harriet E. Townshend 1867–1882
80. Rev. W. E. DeRiemer 1869–1878
81. Mrs. Emily DeRiemer 1869–1878
82. Mrs. Maggie Webster Wood 1869–1869
83. Miss Hester A. Hillis 1870–1880
84. Rev. Thomas S. Smith 1871–1898
85. Mrs. Emily F. Smith 1871–1898
86. Miss Susan Reed Howland 1873–
87. Rev. Samuel W. Howland 1873–1898
88. Mrs. Mary E. K. Howland 1873–1898
89. Rev. Richard C. Hastings 1879–1904
90. Mrs. Minnie T. Hastings 1882–1904
91. Miss Mary Leitch 1880–1886
92. Miss Margaret W. Leitch 1880–1886
93. Mr. Geo. W. Leitch 1880–1882

94. Miss Kate E. Hastings 1882–1891
95. Rev. Ernest A. Bell 1891–1892
96. Mrs. Mary Bell 1891–1892
97. Rev. Thos. B. Scott, M. D. 1893–1913
98. Mrs. Mary M. E. Scott, M. D. 1893–1913
99. Miss Kate L. E. Myers 1893–1898
100. Miss Isabella H. Curr, L. R. C. P. S. 1896–
101. Mrs. Mary Irwin Rutnam, M. D. 1896–1897
102. Rev. Giles G. Brown 1899–
103. Mrs. Clara P. Brown 1899–
104. Miss Annie E. Young, M. D. 1899–1904
105. Miss Helen I. Root 1899–1907
106. Rev. Jas. H. Dickson 1900–
107. Mrs. Frances H. Dickson 1900–
108. Miss Julia E. Green 1906–1910
109. Miss Zillah Scott-Patten 1907–1909
110. Mr. Wm. E. Hitchcock 1908–
111. Mrs. Hattie A. Hitchcock 1908–
112. Mr. Arthur A. Ward 1909–
113. Mrs. Alice B. Ward 1909–
114. Miss Lulu H. Bookwalter 1911–
115. Miss Minnie A. Hastings 1913–
116. Mr. Chas. Miller 1914–
117. Mrs. Edith Gates Miller 1916–
118. Rev. John Bicknell 1915–
118. Mrs. Nellie Bicknell 1915–
120. Miss Lucy A. Clark 1915–